How to Eat Like a Southerner and Live to Tell the Tale

How to Eat Like a Southerner and Live to Tell the Tale

Courtney Parker

FOREWORD BY

Lee Bailey

DESIGNED BY

ALEXANDER ISLEY DESIGN

CLARKSON POTTER/PUBLISHERS

NEW YORK

Published by Clarkson N. Potter, Inc.,
201 East 50th Street, New York,
New York 10022. Member of the
Crown Publishing Group.

CLARKSON N. POTTER, POTTER,
and colophon are trademarks of
Clarkson N. Potter, Inc.

Manufactured in the United States
of America

Library of Congress Cataloging-in-
Publication Data
Parker, Courtney.
    How to eat like a Southerner and live
to tell the tale / by Courtney Parker;
foreword by Lee Bailey.—1st ed.
        p.   cm.
    1. Cookery, American—Southern
style.   I. Title.
TX715.2.S68P37   1992
641.5975—dc20   90-28596
                                                CIP
ISBN 0-517-57683-X

10   9   8   7   6   5   4   3   2   1

First Edition

With affection and huge thanks to my dear friend Lee Bailey, who showed me the ropes and yanked me along when I needed it. To Amy Schuler, a keen editor, whose gentle good nature kept me from hanging myself, and to Shirley Wohl, who tied it all up with a bow. To my agent, Pam Bernstein, for hooking me up with all the nice people at Clarkson Potter. To all the nice people at Clarkson Potter and at Crown: Maria Bottino, Joan Denman, Howard Klein, Susan Magrino, Bill Nave, Carol Southern, and Jane Treuhaft.

ACKNOWLEDGMENTS

A very special thank-you to my family and friends for their encouragement, generosity, and appetites during the testing of these recipes.

To my mother, Hattie Ruder, my cousin, Bonnie Travis, and my pals, Robbie Williams, Guy Bass, and Willie Beth Dees, for acting as galley slaves to my Captain Bligh during the last stages of my pregnancy.

For my husband, Fred, and our son, Stacy, with love

CONTENTS

FOREWORD Toward the end of 1987 I went to Natchez, Mississippi, to put together an article on a typical Southern Thanksgiving feast. I knew there would be magnolias and camellias, corn bread stuffing and cranberries, and local charm and hospitality. But what I didn't know is that there would also be a young Southern belle with chestnut-colored hair and an engaging smile who could cook like a pro—as I soon found she was. And what I also didn't know on that first meeting was that this daughter of Dixie could write like a dream—with a voice as clear as air and as true as blue sky. It's a voice that speaks of small, fleeting moments and re-membered joys, of favorite diversions and local tradition.

Her name is Courtney Parker, and a great deal of what she is concerned with focuses on the indigenous food of her much-loved home place, as it has been prepared in these parts for generations. But when it comes to the way we eat today, Courtney feels it's time to take a second look at these marvelous dishes with an eye to bringing them more in line with what we now consider a heathful way of eating. The result is a mix of innovative methods and sly alterations that make these delicious old standbys kinder to the body while still being true to their soul. I think you'll love what she has done, and if you like to eat this evocative food, she makes it possible to have your mustard greens and eat them, too—without the ham hock.

And even if you don't hanker after new-style gumbo, there's that wonderful voice!

You've got a treat in store. Read on.   **LEE BAILEY**

INTRODUCTION I live in the lower left-hand corner of Mississippi. Yes, indeed, it's hot. I drink Cokes for breakfast and I eat salt pork in my mustard greens. I know who my second cousin three times removed on my maternal great-grandmother's side of the family was, and of what he died. No, I don't think I'll ever leave. That's not to say that I haven't viewed Ol' Man River as an escape route, but for the most part, I view him as home. Natchez, Mississippi, is brimming with extravagance left over from the notorious King Cotton era and I like it here.

Our customs are old and fermented by decades of isolation, and our economic history is as full of twists and turns as the Mississippi River. We may appear to be holding on by our well-worn manicures, yet we continue to kick up our heels at the drop of a sunbonnet. Any event, whether it is a wedding, Ground Hog Day, or a sudden funeral, can turn into an all-night roaring celebration with plenty of good Southern food and open bars.

Food down here is held in reverence. Family recipes for cakes and pies or chicken and dumplings are passed from generation to generation with the loyalty of exact duplication. Gifts of food, such as smoked pork tenderloin or sweet potato pie, are really an offering of heart and soul.

As I was growing up, the kitchen was my favorite room in any house and cooks my favorite people. On my great-grandfather's farm we had a brother-and-sister team of cooks named Monk and Booze. I remember them as being elephantine, frolicsome, and what my great-grandmother, Mama Lady, called sassy. No matter how hot the kitchen or how complicated the recipe, their banter and advice was loud and constant. Like huge, jolly mad scientists, they would scurry-waddle from the sink to the table to the stove, Monk's fat arm flapping as she creamed butter and sugar with nothing but a wooden spoon.

Cooking came naturally to Booze. A mound of sugar poured into his cupped palm would measure an exact tablespoon. He could free-pour buttermilk into a cake batter and know when to stop by the sound. The cake was done when it smelled right and the gravy done when it looked right. He could also tell a story about little of nothing and send me into shaking giggles. These two were my childhood heroes.

My great-grandmother was no novice in the kitchen, either. She was born and reared on a plantation, as were her children and grandchildren. The men in my family raised

cattle and Mama Lady could make use of every speck of a cow. Not only did she make butter, she also made cream cheese and cooked mountain oysters and brains for the men. They must have been real men.

I spent many hours watching and trying to help Mama Lady. My hands-on cooking experience started when she handed me a dull knife, a wooden bowl, and a bunch of fresh parsley. She sat my four-year-old rump down on the kitchen floor and told me that I had a very important task; I must chop this good-smelling green stuff for the family

dinner. In truth, she wanted my greedy hands out of the cake batter. As I sat mutilating the parsley, I noticed the moisture and fragrance released when I tried to chop it or when I made my hairless Barbie doll stomp the young tender leaves. In short, my fascination with food was born through playing with it rather than eating it.

Fried okra, game bird pie, turnip greens, purple hull peas, venison, fried corn, clabber cream cheese, home-cured ham, dewberries: these are some of the foods that I adore. Eating has surpassed my desire to play with food. In fact, I'd rather eat than do a whole lot of things. A deep red, garden fresh, juicy tomato as big as your hand, sliced and spread with plenty of home-made mayonnaise, makes me very happy.

Unfortunately, Southern food has always had a reputation swathed in pork fat, and rightfully so. I found an old recipe for cream gravy that called for "a cup of fat"—not any particular kind of fat, just "a cup of fat." Any vegetable we cook is flavored with salt pork and sugar, we love that deep-fat fryer, and let's not forget those lard-laden biscuits.

My goal is to keep the essence of hearty country flavor in my Southern recipes while cutting down on the sodium, saturated fat, and sugar. I began tinkering with family recipes while studying art and theater in college. Holistic vegetarians were swarming the campus and I jumped in with both feet. After existing on nuts, seeds, and sprouts for a couple of months, I began to crave pork chops and fried chicken. Realizing that a compromise must be reached, I began analyzing our familiar dishes and altering them by substituting strong flavors for strong flavors, like rich chicken stock, garlic, bay leaf, thyme, sage, and red pepper for sausage in a pot of beans.

You will not find calorie counts or clinical discussions of nutrition in these pages. I believe if one has a genuine interest in eating healthful foods, common sense will prevail. And whether you are restricted to a diet for medical reasons or simply watching your waistline, it's much more fun to eat the food because it tastes good, rather than because it has fewer calories or less fat. With well-balanced menus and a healthy dose of moderation we can keep the emphasis on good flavor and enjoyment instead of confusing figures and conflicting reports.

I don't want to see the traditional foods I grew up on fade away like so much cream sauce. I aim to save the soul in Mama Lady's recipe for sweet potato pie and Booze's recipes for biscuits and corn bread while creating healthful recipes that even a Yankee will feel safe in consuming. In the recipes that follow, I have used the same technique, substituting low-fat ingredients for those high in fat and cholesterol. For example, butter has been replaced with margarine, bacon fat with canola oil, heavy cream with low-fat yogurt and light sour cream, whole milk with low-fat milk, homemade mayonnaise with cholesterol-free commercial mayonnaise.

Lighthearted **Beginnings**

D **EEP** South
parties are a combination of Old
World elegance and downright
Southern vulgarity. No other re-
gion displays eccentricity with so

much pride and finesse. Weddings, Confederate balls, and holiday cocktail parties nip in the bud any tendency toward putting on airs, as the guest lists lay wide open our family trees for the rest of the community to dance and drink with, if they dare.

As a caterer, I have enjoyed the vantage point of the proverbial fly on the ceiling fan. I've watched the mayor dribble salsa down his chin, a girdled bride lick the extra mayonnaise from the side of a dainty sandwich, and a veteran party dowager empty a bowl of dip with one chip. I've seen a jeweled oil heiress walk away from the hors d'oeuvre table gesturing with a chicken bone, and as she approached the tiki torches in the backyard, slip the gnawed morsel into her tiny beaded bag. Although these moments feed my sinister sense of humor, I feel it is my duty to prevent them by creating light and elegant tidbits that won't stick to your fingers or to your ribs.

This chapter provides a few alternatives to the miniature fried chicken legs and the ubiquitous layered Tex-Mex dips usually found on Southern silver trays. Bite-size combinations of vegetables, lean meats, and seafood give us a healthful menu for an old-fashioned, hell-raisin' good time.

Stuffed Mustard Greens

**Cauliflower in
Basil Berry Marinade**

Tarragon Shrimp

Eggplant Caviar

Tarragon Carrots

Cheese Pennies

Crawfish Mousse

**Eggplant-Stuffed
Mushrooms**

Lean Pork Pâté

Marinated Mushrooms

Red-Hot Roasted Pecans

**Broiled Oysters
with Champagne**

STUFFED MUSTARD GREENS

This is a Southerner's answer to stuffed grape leaves. Be sure to use the smallest leaves available as large ones will be tough.

50 young, tender mustard green leaves, stemmed and washed (see Note, page 149)

2 tablespoons (¼ stick) margarine

2 cups finely chopped onions

1 garlic clove, minced

½ cup finely chopped pecans

1 cup chopped peeled fresh tomatoes

2 cups rice cooked in Defatted Chicken Stock (page 20)

½ cup minced lean ham

½ teaspoon ground thyme Salt and freshly ground black pepper to taste

Bring about 1 quart of water to the boil and blanch the mustard greens for 45 seconds. Drain and spread out to dry on paper towels.

In a medium skillet over medium-high heat, melt the margarine; add the onion, garlic, and pecans. Sauté the mixture for 15 minutes or until the onion is translucent. Add the remaining ingredients and cook, tossing, for about 5 minutes, until most of the liquid is absorbed.

Place about 1½ teaspoons of the stuffing at the wide end of each mustard green leaf. Fold the sides in toward the middle and roll up the leaf like a bed roll. Stack all of the rolled leaves seam side down in the top of a steamer and steam over low heat for 30 to 45 minutes or until the greens are tender.

Serve hot.

Makes about 50 bite-size rolls

CAULIFLOWER IN
BASIL BERRY MARINADE

~~~~~~~~~~~~~~~~~~~~~~~~~~

Use this cauliflower as a garnish, in a salad, or as part of a vegetable tray.

⅓ cup Blackberry Vinegar
(recipe follows)

⅓ cup canola oil

2 tablespoons chopped
fresh basil leaves

½ teaspoon salt

½ teaspoon freshly ground
black pepper

1 large head cauliflower,
separated into
flowerettes

Whisk together the first 5 ingredients and pour over the cauliflower. Place in an airtight container and refrigerate overnight.

Makes about 40 flowerettes

BLACKBERRY VINEGAR

Fill a 1-quart bottle with about 1 pound of whole fresh blackberries. Pour in distilled white vinegar to cover and seal. Store in a dark place for 2 to 3 weeks before using. When you run out of vinegar, refill the bottle with vinegar and let it sit again. The same berries can be used up to 3 times.

Makes 1 quart

TARRAGON SHRIMP

The last time I served these at a cocktail buffet, I provided long wooden skewers for the guests to spear the shrimp in a large crystal bowl, thinking that the ostentatious length of the skewer would slow down the rate at which this expensive dish was consumed. However, as the crowd grew deeper around the food table, the elegantly dressed socialites were using the skewers to poke past heads and elbows to reach not only the last shrimp in the bottom of the bowl but also the ham and roast beef on the other side of the table. It's a great sign when your cocktail food has the power to reduce people in their best clothes to a ravenous horde. Enjoy!

1 *pound Boiled Shrimp (page 72)*	½ *teaspoon salt*
¼ *cup rice wine vinegar*	½ *teaspoon freshly ground black pepper*
¼ *cup dry champagne*	1 *cup canola oil*
2 *tablespoons chopped fresh tarragon*	1 *cup sliced red onion*
1 *garlic clove, minced*	1 *pint cherry tomatoes*
1 *teaspoon Dijon-style mustard*	

Peel the shrimp and toss them with the remaining ingredients in an airtight container. Refrigerate overnight. Serve at room temperature.

Serves 8

EGGPLANT CAVIAR

This spread is a great base for canapés or a stuffing for vegetables or eggs. It's also delicious on toasted French bread rounds.

1 *large eggplant*	1 *tablespoon extra-virgin olive oil*
¼ *teaspoon salt*	

1 *chopped onion*
½ *garlic clove, minced*
½ *cup chopped red bell*
   pepper
½ *cup chopped peeled*
   fresh tomatoes

½ *teaspoon sugar*
   (optional)
   Freshly ground black
   pepper to taste
1 *tablespoon lemon juice*

Preheat the oven to 400 degrees.

Cut the eggplant in half lengthwise and sprinkle both halves with the salt; let stand for 20 minutes to release its liquid.

Spray a baking sheet with nonstick vegetable coating. Place the eggplant halves skin side down on the baking sheet and bake for 30 minutes or until very soft. Remove the eggplant from the oven; cool and scoop out the pulp. Set aside.

Heat the oil in a medium skillet over medium heat. Add the onion, garlic, and pepper. Sauté for about 10 to 15 minutes, or until the onion is translucent.

Place the eggplant pulp, sautéed vegetables, and remaining ingredients in a blender or food processor and blend until smooth. Adjust seasonings and lemon juice to taste.

Makes about 3 cups

TARRAGON CARROTS

These carrots add an extra zip to salads or a vegetable tray.

1 *pound carrots, scraped*
   and cut into small sticks
⅓ *cup lemon juice*

⅓ *cup canola oil*
2 *tablespoons chopped*
   fresh tarragon

Combine all the ingredients in an airtight container and refrigerate overnight.

Makes about 50 small carrot sticks

CHEESE PENNIES

Cheese pennies attend all Southern parties, weddings, and funerals. They freeze, keep well even in a cookie tin, and taste good with bourbon.

1 *cup grated reduced-fat Cheddar cheese*
⅓ *cup canola oil*
1 *teaspoon salt*

¼ *teaspoon cayenne pepper*
1 *cup all-purpose flour*

Place the cheese in the bowl of a food processor. With the machine running, add the oil, tablespoon by tablespoon. Add the salt, cayenne pepper, and flour all at once. Process until well blended. The mixture should resemble small peas and be quite moist. Gather the dough into a ball and refrigerate for 30 minutes.

Preheat the oven to 350 degrees.

Roll the dough into about 30 small balls and place the balls 2 inches apart on an ungreased baking sheet. Flatten the balls with your palm or press in a criss-cross pattern with a fork. Bake for 12 minutes or until golden brown on the bottom. Remove with a spatula to a cooling rack.

These will keep for about 3 weeks in an air-tight container.

Makes about 30 cheese pennies

CRAWFISH MOUSSE

If you can't find crawfish, try shrimp or lobster. Serve with homemade French bread melba toast made with margarine and garlic.

1   tablespoon canola oil
2   cups chopped red bell peppers
1   cup chopped onion
1   cup chopped celery
1   pound blanched packaged crawfish tails, with their fat (available in some fish markets)
¼   teaspoon ground thyme
2   bay leaves
¼   teaspoon ground oregano
¼   teaspoon cayenne pepper

1   tablespoon Worcestershire sauce
½   teaspoon salt
3   tablespoons lemon juice
1   package unflavored gelatin
¼   cup water
½   cup buttermilk
¼   cup chopped fresh parsley
¼   cup chopped green onion tops

Heat the oil in a large skillet over medium-high heat. Add the peppers, onion, and celery and sauté for about 20 minutes or until the vegetables are soft. Add the crawfish tails, thyme, bay leaves, oregano, cayenne pepper, Worcestershire sauce, salt, and lemon juice. Cook this over low heat, stirring for 10 minutes; discard the bay leaves. Puree this mixture in a food processor until smooth. Set aside.

Sprinkle the gelatin over the ¼ cup water and let stand for 1 minute. Stir over low heat for 5 minutes or until the gelatin is completely dissolved. With the food processor running, add to the crawfish mixture, and then add the buttermilk. Add parsley and onion tops. Adjust the seasonings to suit your taste and pour into a 1-quart mold. To avoid the added calories of buttering the mold, line it with enough plastic wrap to fold back over the bottom. Refrigerate for at least 4 hours before serving. When unmolding the mousse, smooth any wrinkles with a small spatula.

Serves 8

EGGPLANT-STUFFED MUSHROOMS

~~~~~~~~~~~~~~~~~~~~~~

If you're feeling extravagant, add some lump crab meat to this recipe.

2 pounds domestic mushrooms, rubbed clean with a dry paper towel

1 medium eggplant
Salt

1 tablespoon extra-virgin olive oil

½ cup finely chopped onion

½ cup finely chopped green bell pepper

⅛ teaspoon ground oregano

1 tablespoon toasted bread crumbs

1½ teaspoons lemon juice
Freshly ground black pepper

¼ cup grated Parmesan cheese

¼ cup Defatted Chicken Stock (page 20)

Separate the mushroom caps from the stems; set aside the caps and chop the stems. Peel and chop the eggplant. Sprinkle with salt and place on paper towels to sweat for 30 minutes.

Cook the eggplant in boiling water to cover until soft, about 10 minutes; drain and set aside.

Heat the olive oil in a medium skillet; add the onion, pepper, mushroom stems, and oregano and sauté for 15 minutes over medium heat or until the onion is translucent. Stir in the cooked eggplant, bread crumbs, lemon juice, and salt and pepper to taste and cook, stirring, for 10 minutes.

Preheat the oven to 350 degrees.

Stuff each mushroom cap with 1 to 2 teaspoons of the eggplant filling. Place the stuffed caps in a 2-inch-deep baking pan and sprinkle evenly with the Parmesan cheese. Pour the chicken stock into the bottom of the pan. Bake for 20 minutes or until the mushrooms pierce easily with a fork.

Makes about 50 stuffed caps

LEAN PORK PÂTÉ

~~~~~~~~~~~~~~~~~~~~~~

This may be served as a first course or as an hors d'oeuvre with crusty French bread, cornichons, and a good mustard.

½ cup minced onion

2 tablespoons minced
   fresh parsley

2 garlic cloves, minced

¼ cup dry white wine

¼ cup beef consommé

1 teaspoon minced fresh
   thyme leaves

1½ tablespoons minced
   fresh sage

1 bay leaf

½ pound chicken livers

1 pound ground lean
   pork

4 egg whites

½ cup evaporated skim
   milk

1 cup ground pecans

¼ teaspoon ground
   allspice

¼ teaspoon grated nutmeg

¼ teaspoon ground
   cinnamon

¼ teaspoon salt

1 teaspoon freshly ground
   black pepper

Preheat the oven to 350 degrees. Spray a 2-quart loaf pan with nonstick vegetable coating.

Place the first 8 ingredients in a skillet over medium-high heat and sauté for 15 minutes, until the onion is translucent. Remove the skillet from the heat and discard the bay leaf.

Meanwhile, cut away any fat and gristle from the chicken livers.

Place the sautéed vegetables, chicken livers, pork, egg whites, evaporated milk, pecans, and spices in a food processor; process until smooth. Pour the puree into the prepared pan and bake for 1 hour, until a knife inserted in the center comes out clean. Cover the pâté with plastic wrap and place a weight (a brick covered with foil works perfectly) on top. Refrigerate for 6 to 8 hours before serving. Serve at room temperature.

Serves 8

MARINATED MUSHROOMS

~~~~~~~~~~~~~~~~~~~~~~~~~

**These work well as an hors d'oeuvre, a vegetable side dish, or
in place of a pickle as an accompaniment.**

2 pounds domestic
mushrooms, rubbed
clean with a dry paper
towel
⅓ cup dry white wine
⅓ cup white wine vinegar
⅓ cup canola oil

1 tablespoon chopped
fresh oregano
½ teaspoon salt
½ teaspoon freshly ground
black pepper
2 garlic cloves, smashed

Combine all of the ingredients in an airtight container and refrigerate
overnight. Drain and serve at room temperature.

Makes about 40 mushrooms

RED-HOT ROASTED PECANS

~~~~~~~~~~~~~~~~~~~~~~~~~

**I developed this spicy pecan for Lee Bailey's shops at Saks
Fifth Avenue. The original was deep-fried for quick roasting
but this version is much better for you. By the way, "red-hot"
means just what it says.**

3 cups pecan halves
2 tablespoons (¼ stick)
margarine, melted
½ teaspoon ground cumin
½ teaspoon cayenne
pepper, or less for
milder taste

½ teaspoon ground thyme
½ teaspoon grated nutmeg
1 teaspoon salt
½ teaspoon freshly ground
black pepper, or less for
milder taste

Preheat the oven to 350 degrees.

Toss all the ingredients together in a bowl until well coated. Spread the pecans out on an ungreased baking sheet and place in the oven. Bake for 15 minutes or until fragrant; stir often to prevent burning.

Makes 3 cups

BROILED OYSTERS WITH CHAMPAGNE

This needs no more embellishment than perhaps a piece of French bread and a glass of champagne.

2 *dozen oysters, shucked*
½ *cup dry champagne*
¼ *cup grated Parmesan cheese*
¼ *cup minced green onion tops*

1 *tablespoon margarine*
Freshly ground black pepper to taste

Preheat the broiler.

In 8 individual ramekins or custard cups, place 3 oysters in each. Divide the remaining ingredients evenly among the ramekins. This amounts to about 1 tablespoon of champagne, 1 teaspoon of cheese, 1 teaspoon of green onion, and ¼ teaspoon of margarine per 3 oysters. Sprinkle with pepper.

Place the ramekins on a baking sheet. Broil the oysters about 6 inches from the heat for about 5 minutes, or until the oysters puff and their edges curl. Serve immediately in the ramekins.

Serves 8

{ *Soups to* **Warm Your Soul** }

WINTER, in the Deep South, never seems to make it on time. We anticipate cold weather in our shirtsleeves all through the holidays, only to be surprised with ice storms on Valentine's Day. When the winter wind finally does arrive, braced with the ever-present humidity, it cuts through us like a wet blade.

As we huddle together in front of various fireplaces, sipping warm drinks and discussing our power failures and frozen pipes, we have, lo and behold, found ourselves at yet another party. And although a little bourbon goes a long way, this is the perfect time to sit down to a hot bowl of homemade soup.

The next sunrise may bring the temperature soaring to summer heights, so a bowl of chilled soup can be just as comforting in a Southern December.

No matter what the temperature, a bowl of good soup seems to make me feel better. Its restorative powers are presumed even if the base of the soup happens to be flour and hog jowls. Merely passing by the canned soup section in the grocery store gives me a warm feeling. I remember feverish afternoons, tucked in my mother's bed, sipping chicken and stars, nibbling Saltines, and feeling very loved.

The soups in this chapter are both old-fashioned and healthful. I have combined fat-free broths with our favorite vegetables, seafood, and lean meats for new recipes, and I've cleaned up a few of our old favorites as well. I've also given suggestions for accompaniments, but don't feel bound by them—experiment!

Black-Eyed Pea Soup

Potato and Buttermilk Soup

Red Bean Soup with Shrimp

Crookneck Squash and Red Onion Soup

Oyster Stew Without Cream

Corn Cob Soup

Beet and Buttermilk Soup

Chicken Soup with Cornmeal Dumplings

Okra Gumbo

Butter Bean Soup

Oysters Rockefeller Soup

Carrot and Red Bell Pepper Soup

Roasted Red Bell Pepper Soup with Tarragon

Sweet Potato Soup

BLACK-EYED PEA SOUP

Like a Southern debutante, this soup comes from good stock. It can be made a few days ahead and kept in the refrigerator, or frozen. Reheat on top of the stove or in the microwave. Try this soup with Cornsticks with Light Cracklins (page 163).

1 *pound fresh or frozen black-eyed peas*
1 *cup chopped onion*
½ *cup chopped green bell pepper*
½ *cup chopped red bell pepper*
½ *cup chopped celery*
1 *tablespoon minced fresh basil, or 1 teaspoon dried basil*

2 *bay leaves*
8 *cups Good Southern Stock (recipe follows) Salt and freshly ground black pepper to taste*
1 *cup fresh tomatoes, peeled, seeded, and chopped, for garnish*

Place the peas, onion, peppers, celery, basil, bay leaves, and stock in a large kettle and bring to the boil over medium-high heat. Reduce the heat to low, cover the kettle, and simmer for 1½ hours, until the vegetables are soft. Add salt and pepper to taste.

Garnish with the tomatoes. Serve hot.

Serves 8

GOOD SOUTHERN STOCK

This will keep up to 3 days refrigerated, or may be frozen.

3 *pounds chicken wings and backs*
2 *ham bones, trimmed of all fat, cracked in half*
4 *quarts water*
3 *large onions, cut in half*
4 *large carrots, peeled and cut into large rings*

8 *green onions, ragged ends chopped off*
2 *large turnips, cut into quarters*
2 *bay leaves*
8 *large celery ribs, broken into large pieces*
½ *teaspoon ground thyme*

½ teaspoon ground	2 teaspoons freshly
marjoram	ground black pepper
Salt to taste	

Place the chicken, ham bones, and water in a large soup kettle and bring to the boil over high heat. Cook for about 10 minutes, then skim off the foam. Add the other ingredients and bring back to the boil. Reduce the heat to low and simmer very slowly for about 2½ hours.

Strain the cooked stock through a damp cheesecloth-lined colander. Discard the solids, then cool and refrigerate the stock. When the fat has congealed on top, remove and discard it.

Makes 3½ to 4 quarts

POTATO AND BUTTERMILK SOUP

I cook potato soup often in winter for its hearty, "stick to your ribs" quality, but I use buttermilk instead of cream. The buttermilk flavor in the soup is reminiscent of a baked potato with sour cream, but it contains almost no fat and is full of nutrients. Cheese Pennies (page 8) are a crisp counterpoint to this soup.

4 cups diced peeled	1 cup buttermilk
potatoes (about 4 large	1 teaspoon chopped fresh
baking potatoes)	dill, or ½ teaspoon
4 cups diced onions	dried dill
(about 4 large onions)	1 tablespoon margarine
3 cups Defatted Chicken	Salt and freshly ground
Stock (recipe follows)	black pepper to taste

Place the potatoes, onions, and stock in a large kettle and bring to a bubbling simmer over medium-high heat. Cook for about 25 minutes or until the potatoes are soft. Remove the kettle from the heat and pour the contents into a blender or food processor and puree until very smooth. Transfer the puree back to the kettle and add the buttermilk, dill, margarine, salt, and pepper. Simmer for about 5 minutes over low heat until heated through.

Serves 8

DEFATTED CHICKEN STOCK

I've found that anything cooked with canned stock loses its homemade flavor, so I always keep plenty of the real thing in my freezer. Freeze your stock in ice-cube trays, then pop the frozen squares into resealable freezer bags for easy access.

- 4 *pounds chicken wings and/or backs*
- 4 *quarts water*
- 8 *celery ribs, broken in large pieces*
- 4 *medium carrots, peeled and cut into large rings*
- 4 *medium onions, quartered*

- 2 *medium turnips, peeled and quartered*
- 2 *garlic cloves*
- ½ *cup chopped fresh parsley*
- 1 *teaspoon dried thyme*
- 1 *large bay leaf*
- 2 *whole cloves*
- 8 *white peppercorns*

Place the chicken and water in a large stockpot and boil for 30 minutes. Skim off the foam and add the remaining ingredients. Bring the stock back to the boil, reduce the heat to low, and simmer for 3 hours or until reduced by half.

Cool the stock and strain it through a colander that has been lined with damp cheesecloth. Pour the strained stock into an airtight container and refrigerate for several hours until the fat has solidified to form a seal on top. When ready to use, carefully remove the solid fat with a spatula and discard.

Refrigerate stock for up to 3 days or freeze.

Makes 2 quarts

RED BEAN SOUP WITH SHRIMP

This soup is inspired by the popular red beans and rice of Louisiana, in which red kidney beans are simmered for hours with
sausage and traditional Cajun seasonings, then served over rice
for a hearty meal. I have used sausage seasonings instead of the
sausage meat and added shrimp to make a hearty and healthful
soup. I like this soup quite thick but you may add more broth if
you prefer.

1 *pound dried red kidney*
  beans
10 *cups Good Southern*
   Stock (page 18)
1 *cup chopped onion*
1 *garlic clove, minced*
2 *bay leaves*

¼ *teaspoon ground sage*
¼ *teaspoon cayenne*
   pepper
2 *cups small shrimp,*
  peeled and deveined
   Salt to taste

Cover the beans with water in a large bowl and let them soak overnight.

Place the stock, onion, garlic, bay leaves, sage, and cayenne pepper in a
large kettle and bring to a low boil over medium heat. Drain the beans
and add them to the pot. Cover and let simmer over low heat for about
2 hours, or until beans are quite soft. Puree half the beans and stock in
a blender or food processor. Return the pureed beans to the soup and
add the shrimp. Bring the soup back to a simmer and cook the shrimp
for about 5 minutes or until they turn bright pink. Add salt to taste.

Serves 8

CROOKNECK SQUASH AND RED ONION SOUP

~~~~~~~~~~~~~~~~~~~

When crookneck squash is in season Down South, you invariably see it smothered with onions and loads of sweet butter. That version is a real favorite of mine, but for a light summer meal, I have created a soup that keeps the onions and leaves the butter for those who can afford to eat it on their biscuits.

1 *large sweet potato*	1 *teaspoon salt*
2 *cups chopped red onion (about 2 medium red onions)*	½ *teaspoon sugar*
	¼ *teaspoon ground coriander*
8 *cups chopped crookneck squash (about 4 pounds)*	⅔ *cup plain low-fat yogurt*
	1 *tablespoon margarine*
5 *cups Defatted Chicken Stock (page 20)*	

Preheat the oven to 400 degrees.

Bake the sweet potato for about an hour or until quite soft. Set aside until cool enough to handle.

In the meantime, place the red onion, squash, and 3 cups of the stock in a large kettle. Bring it to a bubbling simmer over medium-high heat, then simmer for 25 minutes or until the squash is quite soft.

Scoop out the sweet potato pulp (you should have about 1½ cups) and puree it along with the vegetable mixture in a food processor or blender. Return the mixture to the kettle and stir in the remaining 2 cups of stock. Stir in salt, sugar, and coriander. Simmer on low for 10 minutes until heated through, then stir in the yogurt and margarine. Serve immediately.

Serves 8

OYSTER STEW WITHOUT CREAM

~~~~~~~~~~~~~~~~~~~~~~

To tell you the truth, I was almost reluctant to try a new version of oyster stew since the old standby is so simple and delicious. Real cream and real butter with oysters are hard to beat, but this soup turned out to be just as rich and tasty without all those extra calories. Oyster stew happens to be one of my father's favorite meals, and since he was one of the official tasters for this book, I feel that the way he devoured his portion speaks very highly of my new light version.

4 cups low-fat milk
1 garlic clove
2 cups chopped peeled
    white potatoes
1 cup chopped onion
2 cups shucked oysters,
    chopped into bite-size
    pieces, and 1 cup liquor
    reserved

¼ cup dry white wine
2 tablespoons (¼ stick)
    margarine
    Salt and freshly ground
    black pepper to taste
½ cup chopped green
    onion tops, for garnish

Place the milk, garlic, potatoes, and onion in a large kettle over medium heat and bring to a simmer. Cook for about 30 minutes or until the potatoes are soft. Remove from the heat and puree in a blender or food processor. Return the puree to the kettle and stir in the oyster liquor and the wine. Bring back up to a simmer over medium heat and cook for about 10 minutes. Stir in the margarine and salt and pepper.

About 3 minutes before serving, add the oysters and heat the soup just until the edges curl. Serve in individual bowls, garnished with green onion tops.

Serves 8

CORN COB SOUP

This is a good country soup with a sweet corn broth. Using corn cobs is an old-fashioned, down-home way to give the soup a stronger corn flavor. It is delicious with Grits Soufflé with Parmesan Cheese (page 60) and a green salad.

10 cups Good Southern Stock (page 18)

12 ears of corn, kernels cut off and milk scraped from the cob (about 4 cups kernels), with 6 scraped corn cobs reserved

1 cup coarsely chopped green onions

1 large green bell pepper, coarsely chopped

2 tablespoons Dry Roux (recipe follows)

1 large garlic clove, minced

2 pounds ripe tomatoes, peeled, seeded, and finely chopped

1½ teaspoons salt, or to taste

½ teaspoon freshly ground black pepper

Place the stock and the scraped corn cobs in a large kettle and bring to a simmer over medium heat. Cover and turn the heat to low. Cook slowly for about 1 hour, then pour the broth through a strainer, discard cobs, and set broth aside to cool.

Place the green onions and pepper in the bottom of a large kettle with 1 cup of broth. Cook over medium-high heat for about 25 minutes, until the vegetables are soft. Stir in the roux, and slowly add the remaining stock, blending well with a wire whisk. Add the garlic, tomatoes, and corn with its milk; simmer over low heat for 30 minutes. Add the salt and pepper and serve hot.

Serves 8

DRY ROUX

You can brown just the amount needed for a particular recipe. You can make as little as 1 tablespoon or a large batch to keep in an airtight container. When liquid is added to the browned flour, it turns the rich reddish brown of a perfect roux.

All-purpose flour

Place the flour in a heavy skillet over medium heat. Stir the flour constantly to keep it moving, so it will not burn. The flour will turn a light golden brown after about 25 minutes.

BEET AND BUTTERMILK SOUP

I call this soup my Southern Borscht. I like it served well chilled; if you prefer it hot, reheat it with care over very low heat, since the buttermilk will separate if boiled.

12 *medium beets with stems and leaves*	**7** *cups water*
2 *medium onions, quartered*	**3** *cups buttermilk*
3 *tablespoons minced fresh tarragon, or 1 teaspoon dried tarragon*	**¼** *cup fresh orange juice* *Salt and white pepper to taste* *Tarragon sprigs, for garnish*
½ *teaspoon salt*	

Wash the beets, leaving the stems and leaves intact. Place the beets, onions, tarragon, and salt in a large kettle and cover the vegetables with the water. Bring this mixture to a boil over medium-high heat, then reduce the heat to medium-low and simmer for 1 hour, until the beets are tender.

Remove the beets with a slotted spoon and set aside to cool. Keep the rest of the mixture simmering over low heat for about 45 minutes to concentrate the flavors. When the beets are cool enough to handle, trim roots and stems, then peel them. Puree beets in a food processor or blender until smooth. Remove the broth from the heat and strain it through a colander. Discard the solids, then return the broth to the kettle and stir in the pureed beets, buttermilk, orange juice, salt, and white pepper. Chill the soup thoroughly or reheat it very gently just until steaming. Garnish each bowl of soup with a spring of fresh tarragon.

Serves 8

CHICKEN SOUP WITH
CORNMEAL DUMPLINGS

~~~~~~~~~~~~~~~~~~~~~~~~

This is about as far away as you can get from Southern chicken and dumplings—that incredibly rich concoction full of cream, butter, and flour dumplings. I can eat the original version until I grow into a dumpling, so I limit my intake of it to once every year or so.

Traditional Southern dumplings are a dough made from flour, milk, and lard. The addition of eggs, baking powder, and corn-meal, and the elimination of lard, makes these dumplings very light and melt-in-your-mouth tender.

3 *pounds chicken wings and/or backs*

4 *quarts water*

2 *medium leeks, washed well and cut into large rings*

4 *celery ribs, broken into large pieces*

8 *medium carrots, peeled and cut into large rings*

4 *medium onions, quartered*

2 *medium turnips, peeled and quartered*

2 *garlic cloves*

1 *tablespoon chopped fresh tarragon or 1 teaspoon dried tarragon*

½ *cup chopped fresh parsley*

1 *teaspoon coriander seed*

½ *cup dry white wine*

2 *tablespoons fresh lemon juice*

1 *tablespoon salt*

2 *teaspoons white pepper*

Dumplings

1 *cup yellow cornmeal*

1 *cup all-purpose flour*

1½ *teaspoons baking powder*

½ *teaspoon salt*

1 *tablespoon minced fresh parsley*

2 *eggs*

½ *cup low-fat milk*

1 *tablespoon margarine, melted*

To make the soup, put the chicken wings and backs in a large stockpot, cover with the water, and bring to a boil over high heat. Boil the chicken for about 5 minutes, skim off the foam, and add the leeks, celery, carrots, onions, turnips, and garlic. Lower the heat and simmer very slowly for about 2 hours. Strain the broth and discard the solids. Cool, then refrigerate for several hours or until the fat has solidified.

Remove the broth from the refrigerator and skim off the fat. Return to the stockpot and bring to a simmer over medium-low heat. Add the tarragon, parsley, coriander, wine, lemon juice, and salt and pepper. Simmer the seasoned broth over medium-low heat for about 30 minutes. Meanwhile make the dumplings.

Sift the dry ingredients together into a bowl. Add the parsley and toss to mix. In a separate bowl, beat together the eggs and milk. Make a well in the center of the dry ingredients and stir in the eggs and milk. Stir in the melted butter. The batter will be stiff.

Bring the broth to just steaming and starting to move around a bit but not yet bubbling. Keep it at this state over medium-low heat while the dumplings are cooking, since bubbles will tear the tender dumplings.

Dip a metal teaspoon into the hot broth and then into the batter, retrieving a teaspoonful of batter for the first dumpling. Immerse the batter, still on the tip of the spoon, into the hot broth and push it off with another spoon. The dumpling will first sink, then rise to the top. Repeat this process until the surface of the broth is covered with dumplings— just touching at their edges. Cover the hot broth and allow the dumplings to steam for 15 minutes. Do not raise the lid before 15 minutes has passed. The dumplings will swell. Serve hot with broth.

Serves 6 to 8

Note: If you would like to experiment, try adding your favorite herb to the dumpling batter instead of parsley, and add julienned vegetables to the broth.

OKRA GUMBO

The dark, thick mud at the bottom of the Mississippi River down around Natchez is called gumbo mud, and believe it or not, a good bowl of gumbo should resemble the bottom of the river. You'll be glad to know that's where the comparison ends.

The secret of my gumbo is whole crabs. The flavor hides in the fat right next to the shell, so packaged crab meat just won't do on its own (but that's no reason not to add extra crab meat for a little lagniappe). The small crabs I use are called "gumbo crabs" by Southern fish mongers because they are considered too small to bother with otherwise.

Here I've used Dry Roux to achieve the right consistency and Good Southern Stock instead of ham or sausage for flavoring the broth. And again, Corn Bread (page 167) is the accompaniment of choice.

1 cup chopped onion
1 cup chopped green bell pepper
1 cup chopped celery
1 pound chopped okra
10 cups Good Southern Stock (page 18)
½ cup plus 2 tablespoons Dry Roux (page 24)
1 teaspoon dried thyme
2 bay leaves
¼ teaspoon ground oregano
1 teaspoon paprika
¼ teaspoon cayenne pepper

¼ teaspoon freshly ground black pepper
1½ teaspoons salt
1 cup chopped, peeled tomatoes
4 small gumbo crabs, cleaned and quartered
1 pound shrimp, cleaned and deveined
Dash of Tabasco (optional)
½ pound picked crab meat (optional)
2 cups cooked rice

Place the onion, pepper, celery, okra, and 1 cup of stock in a large kettle and bring to a simmer over medium-high heat. Simmer rapidly for 10 minutes or until onion is wilted. Sprinkle in the Dry Roux and stir well. Whisk in the remaining 9 cups of stock until the mixture is smooth. Add the thyme, bay leaves, oregano, paprika, cayenne pepper, black pepper, salt, tomatoes, and cracked crabs. Simmer for 1 hour over low heat. Add the shrimp and simmer for about 5 minutes or until the shrimp turn bright pink. Add the Tabasco and the extra crab meat, if desired, and serve hot with about ¼ cup of cooked rice in the bottom of each soup bowl.

Serves 8

BUTTER BEAN SOUP

I love butter beans cooked with ham. This soup uses low-fat turkey ham instead of the real thing, and is fortified with Good Southern Stock. It is a hearty soup to build a meal around. Serve with Stir-Fried Greens (page 151) and Yeast Cornmeal Rolls (page 166).

2 *cups chopped turkey ham*
½ *cup chopped fresh parsley*
½ *chopped green onions*
6 *cups Good Southern Stock (page 18)*

1 *pound butter beans (green or speckled), fresh or frozen*
½ *cup chopped fresh tomatoes, as garnish*

Heat a large kettle over medium heat. Sauté the turkey ham to brown lightly, stirring constantly, about 5 minutes. Add the parsley and green onions and continue to sauté over medium heat, stirring constantly for 5 more minutes until the onions are wilted. Pour in the stock and add the beans. Simmer for about 1 hour. (If the butter beans are young and tender, 1 hour should be plenty of time; however, if you are getting rid of some of those big fellows, allow the beans to simmer until they are very tender, adding more stock or water if necessary. This may take up to 2 hours of simmering on low heat.)

Remove the solids from the soup with a slotted spoon and puree them in a food processor or blender. Return the puree to the soup and stir well over medium-high heat. Serve piping hot, garnished with chopped fresh tomatoes.

Serves 6 to 8

OYSTERS ROCKEFELLER SOUP

While reading an old Creole cookbook, I found a recipe that claimed to be very near to the closely guarded secret of the original Oysters Rockefeller at Antoine's Restaurant in New Orleans. Contrary to most claims, this recipe stated that the original contained no spinach but lots and lots of chopped fresh tarragon and seventeen other ingredients. My fondness for the herb bid me to trust this dubious source of information and I created this Oysters Rockefeller Soup. Don't be put off by the amount of tarragon; although the authenticity of the recipe is questionable, the soup is utterly delicious. By the way, I included spinach in my recipe for nutritional strength.

2 tablespoons (¼ stick) margarine

1 tablespoon minced garlic

½ cup minced green onions

½ cup minced celery

2 pounds chopped fresh spinach

6 cups Defatted Chicken Stock (page 20)

2 cups shucked oysters, chopped into bite-size pieces, and 2 cups liquor reserved

1 tablespoon chopped fresh parsley

3 tablespoons chopped fresh tarragon, or 1 tablespoon dried tarragon
Pinch of cayenne pepper
Pinch of grated nutmeg

½ cup dry white wine

Melt the margarine in a heavy soup kettle over medium-high heat. When the margarine begins to foam, add the garlic, green onions, and celery. Sauté for 10 minutes over medium heat, being careful not to brown the garlic. Stir in the spinach and the stock, and cook over high heat until the spinach is quite tender, about 10 minutes. Add the oyster liquor, parsley, tarragon, cayenne, nutmeg, and wine and simmer for 10 minutes. About 3 minutes before serving, add the chopped oysters and simmer just until their edges curl. Serve immediately.

Serves 8

CARROT AND RED BELL PEPPER SOUP

~~~~~~~~~~~~~~~~~~~~~~~~~~~

Red bell peppers added to carrot soup eliminate the need to add any other sweetener. This is a wonderful combination and makes a lovely first course.

4 cups grated carrots
4 large red bell peppers, roasted (see Note), skinned, and chopped
1 cup chopped onion
5 cups Defatted Chicken Stock (page 20)

1 cup low-fat milk
¼ teaspoon ground savory
1 tablespoon margarine
Salt and freshly ground black pepper to taste

Place the carrots, peppers, and onion in a large soup kettle with 2 cups of stock and simmer rapidly over medium heat for 30 minutes, until vegetables are tender. Puree this mixture in a food processor or blender and return it to the pot.

Stir in the remaining 3 cups of stock and the milk. Add the savory and margarine, and simmer over low heat for 20 minutes. Add salt and pepper to taste. Serve hot.

Serves 8

Note: To roast peppers, preheat the broiler. Wash the peppers, cut them in half, and remove the seeds. Place on a baking sheet about 4 inches from the heat and roast for about 15 minutes or until the skins turn black and puff. Remove the peppers from the oven and place them in a paper bag and seal. Place the bag in the refrigerator until the peppers are cool. Remove the peppers from the refrigerator, then peel and chop them. You should have about 2 cups of chopped pulp.

ROASTED RED BELL PEPPER
SOUP WITH TARRAGON

~~~~~~~~~~~~~~~~~~

This soup is a self-indulgent way for me to combine two of my favorite flavors. I am a fool for roasted red bell peppers and tarragon is an herb that my mother used with abandon while I was growing up. I suggest serving this soup in cups because it is quite rich.

1 tablespoon margarine
1 cup chopped celery
1 cup chopped onion
1 garlic clove
1 tablespoon chopped fresh tarragon, or 1 teaspoon dried tarragon
6 cups Defatted Chicken Stock (page 20)

6 large red bell peppers, roasted (see Note, page 31), peeled, and chopped
8 teaspoons light sour cream or plain yogurt, as garnish

Melt the margarine in a large kettle over medium heat and add the celery and onion. Sauté the vegetables for 10 minutes, then add the garlic, tarragon, stock, and peppers. Bring to a simmer and cook for 30 minutes, until all the vegetables are very soft. Remove the garlic clove, and puree the soup in a blender or food processor. Return the soup to the kettle and heat to steaming. Serve with a dollop of sour cream or yogurt.

Serves 8

SWEET POTATO SOUP

"Keep it simple" is the best way to approach a sweet potato. Its luxurious flavor is easily weighed down with extra ingredients, so I added only Oven-Browned Onions to this naturally rich soup. The soup is also good with homemade melba toast, or as my little cousins call it, "Velvet Toast."

4 large sweet potatoes
2 cups Oven-Browned
   Onions (page 152)
8 cups Defatted Chicken
   Stock (page 20)

½ teaspoon salt
½ teaspoon freshly ground
   black pepper
¼ teaspoon nutmeg

Preheat the oven to 425 degrees.

Place the sweet potatoes on a baking sheet and bake them for about 1 hour or until they are very soft. Remove the potatoes from the oven and let them cool for about 20 minutes. When they are cool enough to handle, scoop out the pulp. You should have about 4 cups.

Place the sweet potato pulp, 1 cup of the onions, and 4 cups of stock in a blender or food processor and puree until the mixture is very smooth. Pour the puree into a large soup kettle along with the remaining 4 cups of stock, remaining 1 cup of onions, and the salt, pepper, and nutmeg. Stir the mixture well and bring to a quiet bubble over medium heat. Simmer over medium heat for 20 minutes, until the flavors are well blended. Serve immediately.

Serves 8

Far from
"Garden Variety"
Salads

AS spring rains yield to the warmth of summer, my mind turns to fresh boiled peanuts, tiny butter beans, sweet juicy corn, tender summer squash, and summer fruits such as watermelon, peaches, and figs. Gardens and farmers' markets provide us with an abundance of the season's vegetables and fruits.

This chapter glorifies the seasonal summer harvest with easy-to-make salads. During the steamy months of July and August, cold meat and seafood salads are a staple for most Southerners. I have provided some traditional and some not-so-traditional salads to see us through those months when we just can't bear to get near the stove.

My favorite way to eat fruits and vegetables is straight out of the garden with no frills. However, I have included some light mixes from the garden—and some tasty, low-fat dressings—for those of you who bother to cut them up and eat them with utensils.

I was very excited about the appearance of commercial light and low-cholesterol mayonnaises. These wonders have less fat, but I still believe in using any oil in moderation. The best way to accomplish this for salads is to add the mayonnaise or oil last, tablespoon by tablespoon, until you have just enough to bind the salad.

Hunter's Salad

Marinated Fresh
Corn Salad

Fresh Fig Salad

Country Garden Salad
with Mustard Seed
Dressing

Black-Eyed Pea Salad
with Vinaigrette

Crawfish and
New Potato Salad

Red Bell Pepper Aspic

Pecan Chicken Salad

Butter Bean, Ham,
and Corn Salad

Almond Ambrosia

Slaw with Red Cabbage
and Red Onions

Mustard Seed
Potato Salad

Shrimp Slaw

Apple, Banana,
and Pecan Salad

Snap Bean Salad
with Buttermilk
Dijon Dressing

Wild Rice and Smoked
Chicken Salad with
Blackberry Dressing

Watermelon, Cantaloupe,
and Strawberry Salad

Old-Fashioned
Potato Salad

Crab Meat Salad
with Tomato-Basil
Vinaigrette

HUNTER'S SALAD

This is a wonderful salad for any season. Although I use venison, it works just as well with smoked turkey, leg of lamb, or beef tenderloin.

3½ pounds mixed greens, such as fresh leaf spinach, red leaf lettuce, young small mustard greens, watercress, endive

40 seedless red grapes, halved

1½ pounds rare roasted venison, cut in thin strips

3 tablespoons red wine vinegar

4 tablespoons extra-virgin olive oil

1 teaspoon Dijon-style mustard

1 garlic clove

1 tablespoon chopped fresh chives

2 tablespoons chopped fresh parsley

16 Marinated Mushrooms (page 12) Freshly ground black pepper to taste

Wash and dry the salad greens; arrange on individual salad plates. Divide the grapes evenly among the salads and top with the venison strips.

In a small saucepan, whisk the vinegar, oil, mustard, garlic, chives, and parsley together and bring to a boil. Boil for about 10 seconds, then remove garlic and divide dressing equally between each salad. Garnish each salad with 2 mushrooms and grind black pepper over each to taste. Serve immediately.

Serves 8

MARINATED FRESH CORN SALAD

I like to serve this as a side dish with sliced ham or baked fish. You may vary it by substituting your favorite herb or adding jalapeño peppers and a dash of cumin. Use your imagination!

4 cups fresh corn kernels,
   cut from the cob (6 to 8
   ears)
2 cups chopped fresh ripe
   tomatoes
½ cup chopped red bell
   pepper
¼ cup chopped red onions
2 tablespoons minced
   fresh basil leaves

1 cup olive oil
1 cup white wine vinegar
½ cup white wine
1 tablespoon Dijon
   mustard
½ teaspoon sugar
   Salt and freshly ground
   black pepper to taste

Steam the corn kernels for 2 minutes. Allow to cool then mix with the tomatoes, red bell pepper, onion, and basil. Whisk together the remaining ingredients and pour over the salad. Toss, and refrigerate for at least 3 hours before serving.

Serves 8

FRESH FIG SALAD

Our big, floppy fig trees are usually hidden somewhere around the kitchen door or the back porch. The fruit is coveted for its delicate sweetness. Each summer, I race to my neighbor's yard to beat her and the mocking birds to the first ripe mouthfuls.

This salad is a simple and quick way to get down to the business of eating figs.

2 teaspoons grated lemon
   zest
2 tablespoons honey
4 tablespoons balsamic
   vinegar
4 tablespoons canola oil

4 tablespoons walnut oil
   Salt and freshly ground
   black pepper to taste
2 heads boston lettuce
20 small figs, stemmed and
   peeled

Whisk together the first 4 ingredients, then whisk in the walnut oil. Salt and pepper to taste. Tear small pieces of the lettuce into a salad bowl, and toss with the dressing and figs. Garnish with freshly ground black pepper, if desired.

Serves 8

COUNTRY GARDEN SALAD WITH MUSTARD SEED DRESSING

~~~~~~~~~~~~~~~~~~~~~~~

This salad combines fresh, firm vegetables with a tart dressing. Quantities are not specified; prepare any combination of these or other favorite vegetables as desired.

Cucumber, cut into
½-inch rings
Carrots, peeled and cut
into short sticks
Young snap beans, ends
snapped off and beans
broken in half
Zucchini, cut into
½-inch rings
Yellow crookneck
squash, cut into ½-inch
rings

Celery, cut into thin
sticks
Red bell pepper, cut
into small strips
Green bell pepper, cut
into small strips
New potatoes, boiled in
their jackets
Tomato wedges
Mustard Seed Dressing
(recipe follows)
Lettuce leaves

Toss vegetables together in a bowl, then cover with just enough dressing to coat well. Serve this salad immediately or marinate the vegetables in the refrigerator for a few hours and serve at room temperature on a spread of lettuce leaves. The salad stores well, covered, in the refrigerator for up to 3 days.

MUSTARD SEED DRESSING

1 cup apple cider vinegar
2 tablespoons light brown
sugar
1 tablespoon white
mustard seed
½ teaspoon ground ginger

½ teaspoon cayenne
pepper
4 whole cloves
1 teaspoon celery seed
1 cup canola oil

Place the first 7 ingredients in a small saucepan and bring to the boil over medium-high heat. Boil for 5 minutes, remove from the heat, and cool. Remove the whole cloves with a slotted spoon, then whisk in the oil. Store in the refrigerator in an airtight container.

Makes 2 cups

BLACK-EYED PEA SALAD WITH VINAIGRETTE

The robust flavor of black-eyed peas needs an equally strong gang of vegetables to accompany it. This salad is becoming quite popular and one of my favorite ways to eat black-eyed peas. It is very satisfying.

2 *cups water*
½ *teaspoon dried rosemary*
½ *teaspoon salt*
1 *pound fresh black-eyed peas*
5 *tablespoons Blackberry Vinegar (page 5) or apple cider vinegar*
1 *tablespoon Dijon-style mustard*
¼ *cup canola oil*

½ *cup finely chopped green bell pepper*
½ *cup finely chopped red bell pepper*
¼ *cup finely chopped green onion tops*
Dash of Tabasco
Freshly ground black pepper and salt to taste

Place the water, rosemary, and salt in a small saucepan and bring to a boil. Add the peas and blanch for 10 to 15 minutes or until tender-crisp. Drain the peas and rinse them under cold water.

Mix the vinegar, mustard, and oil. Toss together with the peas, peppers, green onions, Tabasco, and salt and pepper to taste. Marinate overnight. Serve at room temperature.

Serves 8

CRAWFISH AND NEW POTATO SALAD

~~~~~~~~~~~~~~~~~~~~~~~~

This salad uses spicy crawfish tails and plain new potatoes in a fairly traditional rémoulade sauce for a delicious Louisiana conglomeration.

I like to make this salad with spicy crawfish tails left over from a traditional crawfish boil (see below), but you may use blanched packaged tails just as easily. For an extra-spicy flavor, add one package of dried commercial crab boil to the water in which you boil the potatoes.

16 *new potatoes*
1 *teaspoon fresh dill*
2 *teaspoons salt*
2 *cups (about 5 pounds whole) spicy Boiled Crawfish tails, (page 85) or blanched, packaged crawfish tails (available at some fish markets)*
1 *cup chopped celery*
1 *cup chopped red bell pepper*
½ *cup chopped green onions*
2 *tablespoons finely chopped dill pickle*

¼ *cup chopped fresh parsley*
½ *cup light mayonnaise*
1 *tablespoon lemon juice*
2 *tablespoons Creole mustard or any strong grainy mustard*
2 *tablespoons catsup*
2 *tablespoons Worcestershire sauce*
1 *teaspoon Tabasco*
¼ *teaspoon minced garlic*
2 *teaspoons paprika*
¼ *teaspoon salt*
1 *head of lettuce*
16 *lemon wedges, as garnish*

Wash the potatoes and remove any bad spots. Place the potatoes in their jackets, dill, and salt in a large saucepan and cover with water. Bring to the boil and cook for 10 minutes over high heat, until tender. Remove from the heat and allow the potatoes to sit in the hot water for 5 minutes. This keeps them from becoming mushy. Drain the potatoes and allow them to cool. When they are cool enough to handle, skin them if you like and quarter them or cut them into bite-size pieces.

Toss together the potatoes, crawfish tails, celery, bell pepper, green onions, dill pickle, and parsley. Set aside.

In a small bowl whisk together the mayonnaise, lemon juice, Creole mustard, catsup, Worcestershire sauce, Tabasco, garlic, paprika, and salt.

Pour the sauce over the salad and fold to coat the ingredients well. Serve over a spread of lettuce leaves and garnish with lemon wedges.

Serves 8

RED BELL PEPPER ASPIC

The sweet, intense flavor of roasted red bell peppers is unfor-gettable, and this rich aspic will satisfy even their most avid fans, like me.

3 cups chopped peeled
   and seeded fresh
   tomatoes
6 red bell peppers, roasted
   (see Note, page 31),
   skinned, and chopped
1 tablespoon minced fresh
   basil

1 teaspoon salt
½ teaspoon freshly ground
   black pepper
¼ cup dry white wine
⅔ cup orange juice
2 tablespoons unflavored
   gelatin

Spray 8 ½-cup molds or a 2-quart mold with nonstick vegetable coating.

Place the tomatoes and peppers in a food processor or a blender and puree. Transfer the puree to a 1-quart saucepan and add the basil, salt, and pepper. Bring this mixture to a steaming simmer over medium heat and cook for about 5 minutes, until the flavors are well blended.

Mix the wine and juice in a large bowl and sprinkle the gelatin over this mixture. Let sit for a few minutes to soften, then stir the gelatin to dissolve it. Pour the hot puree into the gelatin mixture and whisk until all the gelatin is dissolved. Pour the aspic into the prepared molds and refrigerate for at least 4 hours, until set. Serve cold.

Serves 8

PECAN CHICKEN SALAD

This chicken salad minimizes the amount of mayonnaise used by adding just enough to bind the ingredients.

4 cups chopped boiled chicken

1½ cups chopped celery

1½ cups chopped tart apple, such as Granny Smith

1 cup coarsely chopped toasted pecans

1 cup chopped hard-boiled egg whites (about 4 eggs)

¼ cup chopped green onions

½ cup chopped bread-and-butter pickles

2 tablespoons Creole or grainy mustard

¼ teaspoon salt
Freshly ground black pepper to taste

5 tablespoons cholesterol-free mayonnaise

Toss together all of the ingredients except the mayonnaise. Then add the mayonnaise a tablespoon at a time, until salad ingredients are just bound together. Serve at room temperature.

Serves 8

BUTTER BEAN, HAM, AND CORN SALAD

Small green butter beans or limas are essential for this salad because the speckled or brown varieties are just too tough. Lemon and dill are all this salad needs as a dressing.

4 cups fresh butter or lima beans

2 cups fresh corn kernels

2 cups chopped turkey ham or extra-lean ham

¼ cup fresh lemon juice

¼ cup canola oil

1 teaspoon fresh dill leaves, or more if desired

Salt and freshly ground black pepper to taste

Bring 8 cups of water to a boil and add the beans and corn.

Blanch the vegetables for about 7 minutes, then drain and rinse under cold water. Toss with the remaining ingredients and chill. Serve cold.

Serves 8

ALMOND AMBROSIA

~~~~~~~~~~~~~~~~~~~

Southern holidays are never without the "food of the gods." Like a sweet maiden aunt, Ambrosia appears around Thanksgiving time to flatter the cook and wish everyone good health. It usually stays around until Christmas and then reappears at Easter, but I love it so much that I've decided to keep it around all year long.

My version eliminates the sugar. I keep the simple mixture of pineapple, oranges, coconut, and almonds in the refrigerator to dress up or eat as is at any time.

2 cups chopped fresh pineapple

4 cups halved orange sections, seeds removed (about 6 oranges)

1½ cups shredded fresh coconut

1 cup pitted fresh cherries

1 cup fresh coconut milk

3 tablespoons lime juice

1 cup sliced banana
Almond-flavored liqueur (optional)

½ cup toasted sliced almonds

Combine the pineapple, orange sections, coconut, cherries, coconut milk, and lime juice in a large bowl. If not serving right away, cover and store in the refrigerator. This will keep for 2 or 3 days.

Just before serving, add the banana and toss well. Sprinkle with liqueur (if desired) and top with the sliced almonds.

Serves 8

SLAW WITH RED CABBAGE AND RED ONIONS

~~~~~~~~~~~~~~~~~~

From fish fries to barbecues and picnics, you can find slaw at any outdoor feast in the South. This recipe is especially colorful and delicious.

4 cups shredded red
cabbage,
2 cups grated carrots
½ cup Marinated Red
Onions (recipe follows)
3 tablespoons chopped
sweet pickles

½ cup apple cider vinegar
¾ cup canola oil
2 tablespoons sugar
1 teaspoon Creole or
grainy mustard
Salt and freshly ground
black pepper to taste

Toss the red cabbage, carrots, onions, and pickles together in a large bowl. Place the vinegar, oil, sugar, and mustard in a small saucepan and bring to the boil over high heat. Remove from the heat and pour over the slaw while still hot.

Refrigerate for several hours. Add salt and pepper to taste. Serve cold.

Serves 8

MARINATED RED ONIONS

¼ cup apple cider vinegar
1 tablespoon chopped
fresh tarragon, or
1 teaspoon dried
tarragon
¼ teaspoon salt

Freshly ground black
pepper to taste
¼ cup canola oil
½ pound red onions,
peeled and sliced

Mix the first 4 ingredients in a small bowl. Whisk in the oil and pour over the sliced onions. Refrigerate overnight. I like to keep these in the refrigerator to garnish salads or cooked peas or beans.

Makes about 2 cups

MUSTARD SEED
POTATO SALAD

~~~~~~~~~~~~~~~~~~~~~~~~~~~~~~~~~

You could call this a sort of Southern-style German potato salad. It's served cold and the mustard seeds add a delicious zing to the salad.

6 *medium potatoes*
1 *cup apple cider vinegar*
1 *tablespoon white mustard seed*
2 *tablespoons light brown sugar*
1 *teaspoon celery seed*
4 *whole cloves*

¼ *teaspoon ground ginger*
¼ *teaspoon cayenne pepper*
1 *teaspoon salt*
½ *cup light sour cream*
½ *cup chopped celery*
½ *chopped cucumber*

Boil the potatoes in their jackets, drain them, and let them cool. When they are cool enough to handle, peel and cube them. You should have about 4 cups.

Place the vinegar, mustard seed, brown sugar, celery seed, cloves, ginger, cayenne pepper, and salt in a small saucepan over medium-high heat and bring to a boil. Allow this to boil for 5 minutes. Remove the cloves with a slotted spoon, then pour the dressing over the potatoes and refrigerate for 2 hours.

Just before serving, take the potatoes out to bring them to room temperature, and then toss the potatoes with the sour cream, celery, and cucumber and serve at room temperature.

Serves 8 to 10

SHRIMP SLAW

A summer dinner party down in the jungles of Mississippi calls for a light, cool entrée. This recipe combines the complex flavor of Louisiana spiced shrimp with the hearty texture of a good country slaw.

4 cups shredded green
 cabbage
2 cups grated carrots
¼ cup chopped green
 onions
½ cup chopped toasted
 pecans
3 cups spicy medium
 Boiled Shrimp (page
 72), halved lengthwise

¼ cup Pickled Okra
 (recipe follows),
 chopped
½ cup apple cider vinegar
¾ cup canola oil
1 teaspoon Creole or
 grainy mustard
2 tablespoons sugar
 Salt and freshly ground
 black pepper to taste

Toss the first 6 ingredients together in a bowl. In a small saucepan, whisk together the vinegar, oil, mustard, and sugar and bring to a boil over high heat. Boil for about 10 seconds and pour over the slaw. Add the salt and pepper to taste. Serve immediately, or refrigerate for up to 3 days.

Serves 8

PICKLED OKRA

2 pounds fresh small okra
1 quart distilled white
 vinegar
2 tablespoons salt
1 tablespoon Tabasco
1 tablespoon
 Worcestershire sauce
1 tablespoon dried dill

1 tablespoon white
 mustard seed
1 teaspoon black
 peppercorns
1 teaspoon celery seed
5 whole cloves
5 garlic cloves
5 small chili peppers

Wash the okra and soak in cold water for 1 hour. Sterilize and keep hot 5 1-pint canning jars and lids.

Place all the ingredients except the garlic and chili peppers in a saucepan and bring to the boil. Boil for 5 minutes.

Pack the okra 1 pod up, 1 pod down, in the hot jars and add 1 pepper and 1 garlic clove to each jar. Carefully cover with the boiling liquid and seal. Process for 15 minutes in hot-water bath, then cool. Store in a cool, dry place.

Makes 5 pints

APPLE, BANANA, AND PECAN SALAD

This salad always sat beside the ambrosia on Mama Lady's sideboard. It was her favorite salad and was never excluded from any important dinner. She made it with mayonnaise, but I prefer a lighter version with just a little lemon and honey. In fact, I prefer most fruit salads with just a little lemon and honey.

2 *cups chopped peeled apples*	**1** *cup finely chopped celery*
1 *cup chopped peeled pears (optional)*	**1** *cup coarsely chopped toasted pecans*
2 *cups sliced bananas*	**2** *tablespoons honey*
1 *lemon, cut in half, plus 2 tablespoons lemon juice*	

While chopping the apples and pears and slicing the bananas, squeeze small amounts of lemon juice from the cut lemon on the fruit and toss to coat in order to preserve their appearance.

Toss the prepared fruit with the 2 tablespoons lemon juice and remaining ingredients and refrigerate for up to 24 hours or serve immediately.

Serves 8

SNAP BEAN SALAD WITH BUTTERMILK DIJON DRESSING

This buttermilk dressing is very light and made entirely without oil. You may want to substitute yogurt for the buttermilk if you prefer a thicker dressing.

4 *cups young snap beans*
2 *quarts water*
2 *tablespoons buttermilk*
2 *tablespoons Dijon-style mustard*
2 *tablespoons red wine vinegar*

1 *cup finely chopped toasted pecans*
Salt and freshly ground black pepper to taste

Wash and snap the beans (if necessary). Bring the water to a boil and add the beans. Blanch for 5 minutes, or until tender-crisp. Drain and rinse the beans under cold water.

Mix the buttermilk, mustard, and vinegar in a bowl. Store the beans and the dressing separately in the refrigerator until ready to serve, or toss with the beans and pecans, add salt and pepper to taste, and serve immediately.

Serves 8

WILD RICE AND SMOKED CHICKEN SALAD WITH BLACKBERRY DRESSING

~~~~~~~~~~~~

The dressing recipe was inspired by my friend Lee Bailey's incredible Blackberry Catsup. You can substitute roasted or boiled chicken or smoked turkey for the smoked chicken.

Salad

- **3** cups cubed smoked chicken
- **1** cup chopped celery
- **3** tablespoons chopped green onions
- **2** tablespoons chopped sweet pickles
- **1½** cups cooked long-grain rice
- **½** cup cooked wild rice
  Lettuce leaves

Dressing

- **½** cup blackberries
- **¼** cup Blackberry Vinegar (page 5) or rice wine vinegar
- **1** tablespoon dark brown sugar
  Pinch ground ginger
- **¼** teaspoon ground cinnamon
- **⅛** teaspoon cayenne pepper
- **¼** teaspoon salt
- **¼** cup canola oil

To make the salad, toss the chicken, celery, green onions, pickles, and rice together in a bowl.

To make the dressing, rub the blackberries through a fine sieve to remove the seeds and render the juice and pulp or use a food mill. In a small bowl, whisk together the pulp, vinegar, brown sugar, ginger, cinnamon, cayenne pepper, and salt. Whisk in the oil.

To serve, arrange the chicken mixture on a spread of lettuce leaves and pour the dressing over the salad.

Serves 8

WATERMELON, CANTALOUPE, AND STRAWBERRY SALAD

The simple addition of lime juice to a melon salad is astonishingly delicious.

1 large watermelon	**2** pints strawberries
3 medium cantaloupes	¼ cup lime juice

Cut the watermelon and cantaloupes in half, remove the seeds, and cube the meat. Wash and hull the strawberries, and slice them into bite-size pieces. Toss the fruit in a bowl with the lime juice.

Serves 8 to 10

Note: I have provided the simple way to display this salad. You can, of course, make melon balls, paper-thin slices of melon and strawberry fans, or cantaloupe boats with watermelon sails and strawberry passengers. It's up to you. Just remember to coat all the fruit with lime juice.

OLD-FASHIONED POTATO SALAD

You'll never miss the cholesterol in this adaptation of my mother's potato salad.

6 medium potatoes	**1** tablespoon capers
½ cup chopped sweet pickles	¼ cup light sour cream
6 hard-boiled eggs, whites only	¼ cup cholesterol-free mayonnaise
2 tablespoons chopped green onions	**2** tablespoons Creole or grainy mustard
½ cup chopped celery	Salt and freshly ground black pepper, to taste

Boil the potatoes in their jackets, drain them, and let them cool. When they are cool enough to handle, peel and cube them. In a large bowl, combine the potatoes with the remaining ingredients and fold together with a long-handle spoon. Add salt and pepper to taste. Serve at room temperature or store in the refrigerator until ready to serve.

Serves 8 to 10

CRAB MEAT SALAD WITH TOMATO-BASIL VINAIGRETTE

Fresh crab meat doesn't need much, and this sauce adds just enough flavor to make it really delicious. Not only does this make a wonderful luncheon dish but it's also a great topping for summer canapés.

2 *cups fresh tomato puree*
1 *garlic clove, minced*
¼ *cup chopped green onions*
2 *tablespoons lemon juice*
3 *tablespoons red wine vinegar*
½ *teaspoon Tabasco*
1 *tablespoon capers*
¼ *cup chopped fresh basil leaves*

4 *tablespoons extra-virgin olive oil*
4 *cups lump crab meat, cleaned*
½ *cup chopped celery*
¼ *cup chopped green bell pepper*
Lettuce leaves

Whisk together the tomato puree, garlic, green onions, lemon juice, vinegar, Tabasco, capers, basil, and olive oil. Toss this dressing with the crab meat, celery, and bell pepper. Marinate in the refrigerator for 2 hours.

To serve, drain in a colander and serve over a spread of lettuce leaves.

Serves 8

Omnipresent
Southern Grains

MY Yankee friends recoil in horror at the amount of food I can put away at the crack of dawn. A full Southern breakfast means fried eggs, platters of spicy sausages, crisp bacon or ham, big bowls of fresh berries with cream, piles of hot buttered biscuits with preserves and molasses, sometimes smothered quail, fried squirrel, or oyster omelettes, and always a big helping of grits. The grits they find especially intolerable at any hour. (These are the same women who will linger fashionably over a small luncheon of polenta.)

I guess I never thought about liking or not liking grits. I just ate them as one does toast, with lots of butter. These days I have grits when I can't think of anything else to eat, or when I'm depressed, or when I'm sick, or when I need to feel well fed. I suppose grits exude some kind of comfort, or maybe they just taste good. At any rate, you'll find them in every Southern pantry and on all Southern breakfast tables.

The ubiquitous grits will sometimes ooze their way over to the dinner menu, as a side dish for poultry or pork, especially if there's gravy involved, however rice is the dominant starch after noon. We eat rice with beef, pork, poultry, fish, seafood, and beans, and if there's any left, we save it and make rice pudding for dessert.

Traditionally, grits and rice were prepared blandly to act as a blank canvas or a small "plate well" for holding melted butter or rich gravy. The recipes in this chapter utilize the flavors inherent in these grains, and enhance them with tasty broths, herbs, and vegetables, leaving the butter and fat gravies for those skinny Yankee girls to ladle onto their whipped potatoes.

Cheese Grits

Grits in Bouillon

Rice with Lemon and Dill

Grits Soufflé with Parmesan Cheese

Grits with Spices and Fresh Corn

Red Rice

Okra, Corn, and Tomato Pilaf

Pecan Wild Rice

Rice with Garlic and Herbs

Grits in Skim Milk

Rice-Stuffed Sweet Peppers

CHEESE GRITS

~~~~~~~~~~~~~~~~~~~~~~~~~~~~~~~~~

3½ cups Good Southern
  Stock (page 18)
  1 cup grits
  ½ teaspoon salt
  ½ cup Oven-Browned
  Onions (page 152)
  1 cup grated reduced-fat
  Cheddar cheese

1 cup chopped peeled
  fresh tomatoes
  ¼ cup Light Cracklins
  (page 163)
  1 teaspoon freshly ground
  black pepper
  2 egg whites, lightly
  beaten

Preheat the oven to 350 degrees. Spray a 2-quart baking dish with a
nonstick vegetable coating.

Bring the stock to a boil in a 2-quart saucepan. Stir in the grits and bring
back to the boil. Adjust the heat to low, cover, and simmer, slowly, for
17 minutes or until very thick.

Stir in the remaining ingredients until the cheese is melted and the egg
whites are well blended. Pour into the prepared dish and bake for 1
hour. Serve immediately.

Serves 8

GRITS IN BOUILLON

~~~~~~~~~~~~~~~~~~~~~~~~~~~~~~~~~

**Grits have a tendency to take over a plate, spreading them-
selves slowly and quietly until each bite contains at least one
white grain. This recipe solves that unsightly problem with the
addition of egg whites. When the egg whites are added, the grits
take on a creamy, fluffy texture that makes the presentation of
your hunt dinner or simple family breakfast much more appeal-
ing. You may also add egg whites at the end of any recipe for
grits.**

**The substitution of stock for water eliminates the need to add
butter or too much salt for flavor.**

5 cups Defatted Chicken
  Stock (page 20)
1 cup grits
1 teaspoon minced garlic
  (optional)

2 egg whites
  Salt and freshly ground
  black pepper to taste

Bring the stock to the boil in a large saucepan and stir in the grits and garlic, if desired. Cover, adjust the heat to low, and cook slowly for 17 minutes, or until thick enough for a spoon to leave a deep trail. Whisk the egg whites with a fork or a wire whisk until foamy, then stir into the grits and continue to stir them over the low heat until the grits become light and fluffy, about 5 minutes. Add salt and pepper to taste. Serve immediately.

Serves 8

RICE WITH LEMON AND DILL

The marriage of lemon and dill is a classic, and rice done this way gives a subtle flavor without overpowering your entrée. I like this best with chicken, fish, or seafood.

3 cups water
1 teaspoon salt
1 tablespoon margarine
1 tablespoon chopped
  fresh dill, or 1 teaspoon
  dried dill

1 tablespoon lemon juice
  or 1 teaspoon lemon zest
2 cups long-grain rice
  Freshly ground black
  pepper to taste

Place the water and salt in a saucepan and bring to a boil. Meanwhile, in a 2-quart lidded saucepan, melt the margarine over medium-high heat and add the dill and lemon juice. Sauté for 5 minutes, then stir in the rice until it looks wet. When the water is boiling, add it to the rice, stirring constantly. Cover, lower the heat, and simmer for 18 minutes, or until the rice is fluffy and all the liquid is absorbed. Fluff with a fork and add the pepper. Serve immediately.

Serves 8

GRITS SOUFFLÉ WITH PARMESAN CHEESE

~~~~~~~~~~~~~~~~~~~~~~~~

I developed this recipe as an alternative to old-fashioned baked cheese grits. Cheese grits usually contain lots of whole eggs, butter, and tons of grated Cheddar. Yum, yum, you say? You will find this lighter dish just as yummy!

3½ cups Defatted Chicken
    Stock (page 20)
¾ cup grits

1 cup grated Parmesan
    cheese
5 egg whites

Spray a 2-quart soufflé dish with nonstick vegetable coating. Set aside.

Bring the stock to a boil and stir in the grits. Cover, lower the heat, and simmer over low heat for 17 minutes, or until all of the liquid is absorbed. Place in the refrigerator to cool.

Preheat the oven to 400 degrees.

When the grits have cooled, beat in the Parmesan cheese. Beat the egg whites until stiff peaks form and stir one-third of the beaten whites into the grits mixture. Fold in the rest of the beaten egg whites. Turn the soufflé into the prepared dish and place in the oven. Immediately reduce the heat to 375 degrees and bake for 40 minutes or until nicely brown on top and a knife, inserted, comes out clean. Serve immediately.

Serves 8

GRITS WITH SPICES AND FRESH CORN

~~~~~~~~~~~~~~~~~~~~~~~~

I'm very fond of the combination of grits with corn. The kernels add bursts of moisture and fresh flavor throughout the grits. In this recipe, I've used spices for a Mexican flavor, but experiment with your favorite herbs and spices. I like to serve these grits with a Western omelette or lean pork with its natural gravy, or salsa.

5 cups Defatted Chicken
  Stock (page 20)
1 cup grits
1 cup corn kernels,
  scraped from the cob
  and with milk reserved
  (about 4 young ears)

¼ teaspoon ground cumin
¼ teaspoon cayenne
  pepper
  Salt to taste

In a large saucepan over medium-high heat, bring the stock to a boil and stir in the grits and corn. Cover, lower the heat, and cook slowly for 17 minutes, or until a spoon leaves a deep trail. Stir in the cumin, cayenne pepper, and salt and serve immediately.

Serves 8

RED RICE

~~~~~~

In my opinion, the addition of red bell pepper to almost any dish is an improvement, and this rice recipe is no exception. I like to serve this with grilled fish or seafood.

1 tablespoon margarine
1 cup chopped green
  onions
1 cup fresh peeled
  tomatoes
2 red bell peppers, roasted
  (see Note, page 31),
  peeled, seeded, and
  chopped

1 teaspoon chopped fresh
  marjoram leaves, or
  ¼ teaspoon ground
  marjoram
2 bay leaves
3 cups cooked rice, cooked
  in Defatted Chicken
  Stock (page 20)

Melt the margarine in a large skillet over medium-high heat. When the margarine begins to foam, add the green onions and sauté for 10 minutes or until lightly browned. Add the tomato, peppers, marjoram, and bay leaves and cook over medium heat, stirring constantly for about 15 minutes.

Lower the heat and add the cooked rice. Fluff with a fork until rice is heated through and mixture is well blended. Serve immediately.

Serves 8

Okra, Corn, and Tomato Pilaf

Here we go again with my favorite combination of vegetables! Most cooks down here simmer okra, corn, and tomatoes for a day or two. In this recipe, I have kept the simmering time to a bare minimum to capture the fresh flavors of these vegetables.

This dish makes a light accompaniment to ham or chicken.

2 cups Defatted Chicken
  Stock (page 20)
1 cup long-grain rice
1½ cups chopped fresh okra
1½ cups corn kernels
1 cup chopped peeled
  fresh tomatoes (about
  3 small tomatoes)

½ teaspoon salt
  Freshly ground black
  pepper to taste

In a lidded saucepan, bring the stock to a rolling boil. Add the rice and lower the heat. Cover the saucepan and simmer for 18 minutes or until the rice is fluffy and the liquid is absorbed.

While the rice is cooking, place cut okra in a nonstick or cast-iron skillet over high heat. Stir-fry the okra with no oil until the transparent strings (what Booze called okra "glikker") begin to disappear, about 10 minutes. Be careful not to scorch the okra. Blanch the corn in boiling water for 6 to 8 minutes or until tender and drain.

When the rice is done, stir in the okra, corn, tomatoes, salt, and pepper to taste. Serve immediately.

Serves 8 to 10

PECAN WILD RICE

Wild rice has a very strong flavor so I like to combine it with long-grain white rice. And since wild rice tends to be rather expensive, this is also a good way to take advantage of its flavor without putting a big dent in your grocery budget. The pecans in this recipe are toasted, which gives them an entirely different flavor and leaves a divine aroma in your kitchen.

This recipe works well with any entrée and also as a stuffing for fish or poultry.

4 cups of water (see Note)
1 teaspoon salt
½ cup wild rice
1 cup long-grain rice

1 cup coarsely chopped pecans
Freshly ground black pepper

Preheat the oven to 350 degrees. Spray a baking sheet with nonstick vegetable coating, and set aside.

In a small saucepan, bring 2½ cups of the water to a boil and stir in ½ teaspoon of the salt and the wild rice. Lower the heat and simmer slowly for about 45 minutes, or until the grains begin to burst. About halfway through the cooking time, bring the remaining 1½ cups of water to the boil in a separate saucepan, then add the remaining ½ teaspoon of salt and the long-grain rice. Lower the heat, cover, and simmer for 18 minutes.

Spread the pecans on the prepared baking sheet and bake for about 10 minutes or until fragrant. Stir occasionally to prevent burning and for even toasting. Remove from the oven and set aside.

When each rice is done, drain and toss together with the toasted pecans. Add salt and pepper to taste. Serve immediately.

Serves 8

Note: Substitute Defatted Chicken Stock (page 20) for water, if desired.

RICE WITH GARLIC AND HERBS

~~~~~~~~~~

Rice with butter or gravy or both has long been a staple Down South, especially near and in Louisiana. Although rice is not high in fat, the butter and gravy will get you in the end.

This recipe is delicious without anything extra. Try serving it with Oven-Fried Chicken (page 96) or as an accompaniment to Barbecued Shrimp (page 78).

3 cups Defatted Chicken
  Stock (page 20)
1 tablespoon margarine
1 garlic clove
1 tablespoon chopped
  fresh basil leaves, or
  1 teaspoon dried basil
  leaves

2 cups long-grain rice
  Salt and freshly ground
  black pepper to taste

Place the stock in a saucepan and bring to the boil. Meanwhile, in a 2-quart lidded saucepan, melt the margarine over medium heat and add the garlic clove and basil. Sauté for 5 minutes, then discard the garlic and stir in the rice until the grains take on a wet look. When the stock is boiling, pour it in slowly, stirring constantly. Cover the saucepan and lower the heat. Simmer for 18 minutes, or until the rice is fluffy and all the liquid is absorbed. Add salt and pepper and fluff with a fork. Serve immediately.

Serves 8

GRITS IN SKIM MILK

~~~~~~~~~~

This recipe renders a delicious, creamy version of our all-time breakfast favorite.

5 cups skim milk
1 cup grits

½ teaspoon salt

Bring the milk to the boil slowly over medium-low heat in a heavy saucepan. Stir in the grits and salt. Cover and adjust the heat to low. Simmer the grits slowly for 17 minutes, or until thick enough for a spoon to leave a deep trail. Remove from the heat and serve.

Serves 8

RICE-STUFFED SWEET PEPPERS

I've left this recipe simple enough to serve as a side dish, but you can add seafood, lean ham, or chicken to it and have a meal in a pepper.

3½ cups Defatted Chicken
   Stock (page 20)
1 tablespoon margarine
½ cup chopped green
   onions
1 garlic clove
2 sprigs thyme, or
   ½ teaspoon dried thyme

½ bay leaf
2 cups long-grain rice
   Tabasco to taste
3 tablespoons grated
   Parmesan cheese
½ teaspoon salt
8 small or 4 medium red
   bell peppers

Preheat the oven to 400 degrees. Spray a covered shallow baking dish with nonstick vegetable coating and set aside.

In a saucepan, bring 3 cups stock to the boil. Meanwhile, melt the margarine in a large saucepan over medium heat and add the green onions, garlic, thyme, and bay leaf. Sauté for 10 minutes, then add the rice. Stir until all the grains look wet. Pour in the hot stock slowly, stirring constantly. Cover, lower the heat, and simmer for 18 minutes, or until the rice is fluffy and all the liquid is absorbed. Remove from the heat, fluff rice with a fork, and stir in the Tabasco, Parmesan cheese and salt. Set aside.

Remove the stem end, core, and seeds from each pepper if they are small, or cut them in half lengthwise and remove the seeds if they are large. Fill each pepper cup with the rice mixture and place in the prepared dish. Pour the remaining ½ cup of stock into the bottom of the dish. Cover with foil and bake for 30 minutes, or until peppers are soft.

Serves 8

From Frogs Legs
to Flounder

SUMMER mornings with my husband, Fred, are spent paddling around a pond in a tiny green fishing boat, with our rods and reels cocked, waiting to find that bed of hungry white perch or bream. I wear my lucky fishing hat (to cover the 5 A.M. hairdo), my snakeproof penny loafers, and rubber gloves. When we were first married, Fred would bait my hook and remove the caught fish, but those days are long gone; hence, the gloves. We have glorious times reeling in large and small fish, logs, and lily pads. It's very quiet except for guttural comments from frogs and the chirping of our caged crickets.

As we glide silently toward a particularly "fishy" looking thicket of tall weeds and rotting limbs, the July sun peeks through a merciful cloud cover, and I can see Fred clearly. He looks as silly as I do. He always wears a dew rag tied around his head, long tropical print shorts, and bait-shop sunglasses.

I hear the whiz of his reel as he casts straight and clean for a long distance, then the plop of the minnow as it hits the water. He winds the line in slowly, evenly, and silently, trailing the live bait deep in the pond. Suddenly he jerks the pole straight up and laughs out loud, reeling furiously, the pole bending perilously, the rushes quivering as the snared bream seeks shelter. It's a fun way to get up with the sun, although sometimes I'm not sure whether I feel peaceful or predatory.

Home with a long stringer of trophies, Fred deftly cleans

Jambalaya

Boiled Shrimp

Pecan-Mustard Baked Catfish

Grilled Tuna Steaks with Lemon and Dill

Corn Bread Baked Catfish

Frogs Legs with Tomato-Caper Sauce

Shrimp Creole

Barbecued Shrimp

Grilled Swordfish Steaks with Bell Pepper Salsa

Crawfish Etouffée

Oyster and Shrimp Dirty Rice

Shrimp and Rice Stuffed Flounder

Grilled Soft-Shell Crabs

Spicy Grilled Freshwater Bass

Boiled Crawfish

and filets the fish, sending up a shower of iridescent scales on the back porch. Meanwhile, in the kitchen, I mix the cornmeal with plenty of salt and black pepper, and the milk with Tabasco. Largemouth bass and perch are cut into fat pieces while bream are left whole, bone in. The fish is soaked in milk, dusted with cornmeal, salted and peppered generously, and dropped into a kettle of hot oil. It needs only seven to ten minutes of cooking, Fred standing over the bubbling oil, shifting from foot to foot, waiting for that precise moment when the fish are golden brown on all sides. We eat the crisp, flaky fish with homemade tartar sauce, fried dill pickles, and hushpuppies. Best of all is the light, brittle tail end of the bream, which Fred always saves for me, promising with mirth that it will improve my rhythm on the dance floor.

Any fish—small delicate white perch, magnificent river catfish—or even frogs legs are fried in this old-fashioned manner Down South. They taste light and crisp, but are loaded with extra calories. And, let's face it, they all taste the same. In this chapter, you will find recipes for not only indigenous freshwater fish and shellfish but also their saltwater cousins. I offer a variety of lighter cooking methods and recipes based on Southern seasonings but cooked with only a tiny amount of butter and oil.

JAMBALAYA

~~~~~~~~~~~~~~~~~~~~~~~~~~

Jambalaya is a Louisiana casserole using the week's worth of leftover meats. It may include anything from shrimp to rabbit and usually contains three different kinds of meats. In this version I have used turkey sausage to impart a rich flavor, but very lean ham would work as well.

2 tablespoons canola oil
1 cup chopped onion
¾ cup chopped green bell pepper
¾ chopped celery
1 tablespoon chopped fresh parsley
1 garlic clove, minced
1 pound smoked turkey sausage, cut into bite-size pieces
1 cup chopped cooked chicken
1 pound blanched packaged crawfish tails, with their fat (available at some fish markets)

1½ cups chopped peeled fresh tomatoes
1 cup rice
1½ cups Defatted Chicken Stock (page 20)
1 teaspoon Tabasco
½ teaspoon ground thyme
¼ teaspoon freshly ground black pepper
1 bay leaf
Salt to taste

In a large Dutch oven, heat the oil over low heat. Add the the onion, pepper, celery, parsley, and garlic. Cover and simmer over low heat for 20 minutes, or until the vegetables are soft.

Cook the sausage in a 10-inch skillet over medium-high heat for 20 minutes, stirring occasionally to keep it from scorching. Drain well on paper towels.

Add the drained sausage and the rest of the ingredients to the simmering vegetables and toss until well mixed. Bring to a boil over medium-high heat, reduce the heat to low, and simmer, covered, for 50 minutes or until rice is done, stirring every now and then to facilitate even cooking. Serve hot with crusty French bread.

Serves 8

BOILED SHRIMP

~~~~~~~~

The spicy broth gives the shrimp a great flavor.

2 green bell peppers,
  cored, seeded, and
  quartered
2 red bell peppers, cored,
  seeded, and quartered
2 large red onions, peeled
  and quartered
8 celery ribs, broken into
  large pieces
8 large garlic cloves
8 lemons, quartered
4 bay leaves
2 tablespoons chopped
  fresh thyme, or
  1 teaspoon dried

2 tablespoons chopped
  fresh oregano, or
  1 teaspoon dried
1 teaspoon cayenne
  pepper, or more if
  desired
1 cup chopped fresh
  parsley
6 whole cloves
2 tablespoons salt
12 quarts water
4 pounds medium shrimp

In a large kettle, simmer all the ingredients but the shrimp on low for 1 hour. Add the shrimp, cover, and turn off the heat. Allow the shrimp to steep for 10 to 12 minutes, or until pink. Drain and cover the shrimp with ice to retard the cooking. Serve warm or cold.

Serves 8

PECAN-MUSTARD BAKED CATFISH

~~~~~~~~

Delicious pond-raised catfish are now farmed all over the Deep South. Acres and acres of pristine catfish environments are tended by the combination scientist-outdoorsman-farmer. The result is a nonpolluted, freshwater fish of invariably good quality. Southern restaurants now present catfish in new and imaginative dishes, leaving the deep-fat fryer unplugged.

½ cup grainy mustard	Salt and freshly ground
¼ cup canola oil	black pepper to taste
1½ cups shelled pecans	8 catfish filets, 5 ounces
1 teaspoon ground thyme	each
2 garlic cloves	

Preheat the oven to 400 degrees. Spray a baking sheet with nonstick vegetable coating.

Place the first 6 ingredients in a food processor and process until smooth. Spread on both sides of the filets and place the filets on the prepared pan. Bake for 10 minutes or until the fish is flaky and opaque.

Serves 8

GRILLED TUNA STEAKS WITH LEMON AND DILL

Use any leftovers for an incomparable tuna salad.

8 2-inch-thick tuna steaks, ½ pound each	½ cup lemon juice
3 tablespoons olive oil	4 tablespoons fresh dill

Rub each steak on both sides with olive oil and lemon juice and sprinkle with dill. Refrigerate for at least 1 hour.

Make a fire in a barbecue grill with 5 pounds of charcoal and burn the coals for about 30 minutes, to about 400 degrees or until you can hold your palm over the grid for 2 seconds. Set the temperature on a gas grill at 375 degrees. Oil the grid and place the tuna about 6 inches over the coals. Grill for 10 minutes on each side. Serve immediately.

Serves 8

CORN BREAD BAKED CATFISH

In the summers of my childhood, not a week went by without a fish fry. Admittedly, there is nothing like cornmeal-coated, deep-fried filets, yet I have found a delicious substitute that eliminates all the grease but keeps the hearty cornmeal flavor and featherweight texture.

½ cup all-purpose flour
1 teaspoon salt
1 teaspoon freshly ground black pepper
1 egg white
1 teaspoon Tabasco

½ cup buttermilk
4 cups Buttermilk Corn Bread crumbs (page 159)
8 catfish filets, 5 ounces each

Preheat the oven to 425 degrees.

Mix the flour, salt, and pepper on a piece of wax paper. Beat the egg, Tabasco, and buttermilk together in a small mixing bowl. Place the corn bread crumbs on another piece of wax paper.

Coat each filet lightly with the flour mixture and shake off the excess. Dip the floured filets into the milk mixture and allow the excess to drip back into the bowl. Press the wet filets into the bread crumbs firmly, coating on both sides.

Place a footed grid or cake rack large enough to hold the filets on a baking sheet. Place the coated filets fairly close together on the rack and put in the oven. Bake for 10 to 15 minutes, or until the fish is flaky and opaque. Serve with Yogurt Tartar Sauce or Roasted Red Bell Pepper Catsup (recipes follow).

Serves 8

YOGURT TARTAR SAUCE

1 cup plain low-fat yogurt
2 tablespoons minced
  sweet pickles
2 tablespoons minced
  capers
2 tablespoons minced
  green onions
1 teaspoon minced green
  olives

½ teaspoon minced fresh
  tarragon
½ teaspoon dry mustard
1 teaspoon salt
½ teaspoon black pepper
1 teaspoon Worcestershire
  sauce

Stir together all of the ingredients in a small bowl and store, covered, in the refrigerator overnight.

Makes about 1 cup

ROASTED RED BELL PEPPER CATSUP

2 cups chopped roasted
  red bell peppers (about
  6 large peppers; see
  Note, page 31)
¼ cup Oven-Browned
  Onions (page 152)
¼ cup apple cider vinegar
1 tablespoon dark brown
  sugar

¼ teaspoon ground
  cinnamon
¼ teaspoon ground ginger
⅛ teaspoon salt, or to taste
¼ teaspoon cayenne
  pepper

Place the red peppers and onions in the bowl of your food processor and puree. Pour the puree into a small saucepan with the rest of the ingredients and bring to a simmer over medium heat while stirring to prevent scorching. Cook for about 10 minutes, or until all the sugar has melted and the mixture has thickened slightly. Store in an airtight jar in the refrigerator.

Makes 2 cups

FROGS LEGS WITH TOMATO-CAPER SAUCE

For those of you who have never had the courage to taste frogs legs, imagine an aquatic rabbit. Or, to put it simply, they taste sort of like chicken—about as much as rabbit tastes like chicken.

2 cups buttermilk	1 cup all-purpose flour
4 tablespoons Tabasco	1½ teaspoons salt
3 tablespoons chopped fresh basil leaves	1½ teaspoons freshly ground black pepper
2 garlic cloves, cut in half	1 tablespoon canola oil
8 pairs of frogs legs (about 8 pounds)	1 tablespoon margarine

Mix the buttermilk, Tabasco, 1 tablespoon of the basil, and garlic and pour over the frogs legs. Refrigerate overnight.

Separate the frogs legs at the connecting joints and set aside.

Mix the flour, salt, pepper, and remaining 2 tablespoons basil. Place a sheet of wax paper close to the stove. Spread the flour mixture on the waxed paper. Heat the oil and margarine over medium-high heat in a nonstick skillet until the margarine begins to foam. Dredge each leg in the flour mixture and place fairly close together in the hot oil. Pan-fry the legs for approximately 10 minutes on each side or until nicely browned all over. Drain well on paper towels and serve with Tomato-Caper Sauce (recipe follows).

Serves 8

TOMATO-CAPER SAUCE

1 cup chopped peeled tomatoes	1 tablespoon chopped fresh basil
½ teaspoon mashed roasted garlic (see Note)	2 teaspoons lemon juice Scant ¼ teaspoon salt, or to taste
1 teaspoon capers	

Place all of the ingredients in a food processor or blender and process until very smooth. Serve at room temperature.

Makes about 1 cup

Note: To roast garlic, place 3 unpeeled cloves in a 350 degree oven for 15 minutes or until they are soft. Spoon the garlic pulp out of the peel and discard peels.

SHRIMP CREOLE

A Creole sauce is a fine balance among tomatoes, roux, and spices. This is an oil-free mixture and one that I think you will find not only light but well balanced.

2 garlic cloves, minced	**1** teaspoon dried oregano
2 cups chopped onions	**1** bay leaf
2 cups chopped green bell peppers	**½** cup Dry Roux (page 24)
2 cups chopped celery	**2** teaspoons Worcestershire sauce
2 tablespoons Defatted Chicken Stock (page 20)	**12** drops Tabasco, or to taste
2 quarts chopped peeled tomatoes (about 16 very ripe tomatoes)	**4** cups peeled medium shrimp
½ teaspoon dried thyme	**½** teaspoon salt, or to taste
½ teaspoon dried marjoram	

Place the garlic, onions, peppers, celery, and stock in a large, heavy pot over medium heat and sauté for 15 minutes. Add the tomatoes, thyme, marjoram, oregano, and bay leaf and continue to cook over medium heat for 20 minutes.

Stir in the roux, Worcestershire sauce, and Tabasco and simmer for 10 minutes. Add the shrimp and cook for 5 minutes. Season with salt, then serve over rice.

Serves 8

BARBECUED SHRIMP

~~~~~~~~~~~~~~~

Usually recipes for this dish begin with "Melt 2 sticks of butter," and they end with "Use the loaf of French bread to sop up
the sauce." This recipe combines the traditional seasonings
with a reasonable amount of light oil so you don't end up with
butter on your chin or pounds on your thighs.

48 *large shrimp*
1 *cup canola oil*
1 *teaspoon ground thyme*
2 *teaspoons cayenne*
  pepper
2 *teaspoons salt*
2 *tablespoons*
  Worcestershire sauce

½ *cup lemon juice*
1 *teaspoon ground*
  oregano
4 *garlic cloves, minced*
2 *tablespoons paprika*

Peel and devein the shrimp. Mix the remaining ingredients in a large
bowl and add the shrimp. Cover and refrigerate for at least 3 hours or
overnight.

Preheat the broiler. Place the shrimp and the marinade in a baking dish
large enough to hold the shrimp in one layer. Place the baking dish in
the oven and broil the shrimp for 3 minutes on each side.

Or, build a fire in a barbecue grill with 5 pounds of charcoal. Burn the
coals for 20 minutes, or until you can hold your palm over them for 2
seconds. If you have a gas grill, set the temperature to 400 degrees or
medium high. Brush the grid lightly with canola oil. Skewer the shrimp
(6 shrimp on each skewer) and place on the grid. Grill for 3 minutes on
each side, basting frequently with the marinade.

Serves 8

GRILLED SWORDFISH STEAKS WITH BELL PEPPER SALSA

~~~~~~~~~~~~~~~~~~~~~~~~~~~~~~~~~

If you are trying to back off from red meats, swordfish is the perfect choice when you would really rather have a steak. Its meaty texture and rich flavor blossom on an outdoor grill.

8 *swordfish steaks,*
½ pound each

8 *generous slices garlic*

¼ *cup olive oil*

3 *tablespoons freshly ground black pepper*

1 *teaspoon ground cumin*

Pepper Salsa

2 *cups coarsely chopped green bell peppers (about 5 large peppers)*

1 *cup coarsely chopped peeled fresh tomatoes (about 2 medium tomatoes)*

2 *jalapeño peppers, seeded*

2 *tablespoons coarsely chopped green onions*

2 *tablespoons fresh lime juice*

1 *teaspoon sugar*

½ *teaspoon salt*

To prepare the swordfish, rub each steak on both sides with the garlic slices. Divide the oil among the steaks, coating each with about 2 teaspoons of oil. Mix the pepper and cumin and rub on both sides of the fish. Refrigerate for at least 1 hour.

Make the salsa. Place all the ingredients in a food processor or blender and pulse until the mixture is well blended but still in fairly large pieces. Store in an airtight jar in the refrigerator until ready to use.

Make a fire in a barbecue grill with 5 pounds of charcoal. Burn the coals for about 30 minutes, or until you can hold your palm over the heat for 2 to 3 seconds. Brush the grill with canola oil. Set the temperature on a gas grill at 375 degrees. Place the swordfish directly over the hot coals and grill 5 minutes per side, until flaky and opaque throughout.

Serve immediately with the salsa.

Serves 8

CRAWFISH ETOUFFÉE

For those of us without butane crawfish boilers in our backyards, crawfish tails are also sold peeled, blanched, and packed
in ice. This is the best way to buy crawfish since they do not
freeze well, and a sack of live crawfish can be rather messy.
Shrimp may be substituted.

8 tablespoons (1 stick)
   margarine
2 cups minced onions
2 cups minced green bell
   peppers
2 cups minced celery
1 garlic clove, minced
1 teaspoon dried thyme
1 teaspoon dried
   marjoram
1 teaspoon dried oregano

3 bay leaves
2 pounds crawfish tails,
   with their fat (available
   packaged at some fish
   markets)
1 cup Defatted Chicken
   Stock (page 20)
2 teaspoons Tabasco
1 teaspoon salt
1 teaspoon freshly ground
   black pepper

Melt the margarine in a large skillet over medium-low heat and add the
onions, peppers, celery, and garlic. Sauté for about 30 minutes or until
the vegetables are quite soft. Add the herbs, crawfish tails, and stock,
and simmer for 15 minutes.

With a slotted spoon, remove the crawfish mixture and press with the
back of another spoon to push all the liquid back into the skillet. Set the
crawfish mixture aside.

Increase the heat to high and bring the liquid to a boil. Reduce the
liquid by half. Lower the heat, return the crawfish mixture to the skillet,
and add the Tabasco, salt, and pepper. Serve immediately over rice.

Serves 8 to 10

OYSTER AND SHRIMP DIRTY RICE

~~~~~~~~~~~~~~~~~~~~~~~~

Dirty rice gets its name from its color. Traditionally, this dish is made with ground beef and pork, and served as a dressing with poultry and pork. Not only is this seafood variation a nicer color, but its flavor is much lighter and the dish is easier on the digestive system. This can be served as a side dish or an entrée.

2 tablespoons Defatted Chicken Stock (page 20)

1 tablespoon margarine

1 cup minced onion

1 garlic clove, minced

1 cup chopped celery

⅔ cup chopped green bell pepper

2 cups chopped peeled fresh tomatoes

½ teaspoon dried thyme

½ teaspoon dried oregano

½ teaspoon salt

¼ teaspoon cayenne pepper

2 cups coarsely chopped shucked oysters (about ½ pound oysters), with 1 cup liquor reserved

2 cups coarsely chopped peeled and deveined shrimp

1 cup chopped green onion tops

3 cups cooked rice, cooked in Defatted Chicken Stock (page 20)

Place the stock and margarine in a large skillet over medium-high heat. As the margarine melts, add the onion, garlic, celery, pepper, tomatoes, thyme, oregano, salt, and cayenne pepper and sauté for 5 minutes. Add the oyster liquor, increase the heat to high, and cook for about 10 minutes. Lower the heat to medium and stir in the shrimp, oysters, green onions, and rice. Cook, stirring with a fork, for about 5 to 7 minutes or until the shrimp are bright pink and the oysters are plump. Add salt, pepper or herbs to taste.

Serves 8

Note: Substitute other chopped raw seafood such as scallops or crawfish tails if you like.

SHRIMP AND RICE
STUFFED FLOUNDER

~~~~~~~~~~~~~~~~~~

Southern-style stuffed flounder is usually packed with a bread stuffing that seems to be laid in with a trowel, and topped with a cream sauce that stands at attention between the tines of your fork. Who needs the added calories of the fish?

This recipe is very light and actually allows one to taste the delicate meat of the flounder.

Stuffing

1 tablespoon canola oil
1 cup chopped green onions
1 cup chopped celery
1 cup chopped fresh parsley
1 cup chopped red bell pepper
1 teaspoon minced garlic
1 bay leaf
4 cups coarsely chopped peeled shrimp

1 tablespoon chopped fresh thyme
1 tablespoon chopped fresh oregano
4 cups cooked rice, cooked in Defatted Chicken Stock (page 20)
½ teaspoon salt
1 teaspoon freshly ground black pepper

Flounder

8 flounder, cleaned and heads removed
2 lemons, halved
Freshly ground black pepper

Salt
Ground thyme
2 cups sliced onions
1 cup dry white wine

Heat the oil in a medium skillet over medium heat. Add the green onions, celery, parsley, pepper, garlic, and bay leaf. Sauté for 10 minutes, then add the shrimp, thyme, and oregano and sauté for 3 more minutes. Remove from the heat and add the rice, salt and pepper. Set aside while you prepare the flounder.

Preheat the oven to 350 degrees.

Cut each flounder vertically down the center of the dark side, leaving ½ inch to spare on each end. Insert the knife carefully and open the cavity by cutting along the bones as if fileting the fish. You should end up with a large pocket on the dark side of the flounder.

Sprinkle each fish inside and out with lemon juice and pepper, a pinch of salt, and thyme. Fill each cavity with ½ cup of the stuffing. Place the onion slices on the bottom of a baking dish large enough to hold all of the flounder. Pour the wine in the bottom of the dish and bake uncovered for 20 minutes or until the fish is flaky and opaque.

Serves 8

GRILLED SOFT-SHELL CRABS

These are crabs caught with their pants down, so to speak. Soft-shell crabs are caught during the molting season before they grow another shell. The entire crab is edible. This is hard to accept the first time one is placed before you with all of its legs and claws, but after you've eaten four or five of the sweet, buttery-tasting creatures, their embarrassing appearance is soon forgotten.

1 *quart buttermilk*	5 *tablespoons freshly*
1 *tablespoon chopped*	*ground black pepper*
fresh basil	5 *tablespoons paprika*
16 *soft-shell crabs*	*Lemon wedges*
Canola oil, for grill	

Mix the buttermilk and basil in a large bowl and add the crabs. Cover and refrigerate for about 3 hours.

Make a fire in a barbecue grill with 5 pounds of charcoal. Burn the coals for 20 minutes or until you can hold your palm over them for 2 seconds. If you are using a gas grill, set the temperature at 400 degrees or medium-high heat.

Brush the grid with canola oil. Drain the crabs and sprinkle both sides with pepper and paprika. Grill the crabs over the hot coals for 3 minutes on each side. Serve with lemon wedges.

Serves 8

SPICY GRILLED FRESHWATER BASS

~~~~~~~~~~~~~~~~~~~~~~

The first time my husband, Fred, took me fishing, I hooked what I thought was a log. I drearily asked him to free my hook one more time. An avid fisherman of this particular pond, Fred re-alized at once that I had hooked the biggest, eldest bass, which he had been trying to land for two years.

Excited beyond normal boatmanship, Fred literally ran from his end of the fourteen-foot jonboat over to my end. With child-like glee, he forgot the net and pulled my line straight up to get a good look at this old man bass. As the enormous mouth emerged from the water, the veteran fish merely rubbed his teeth against the line with one deft motion, then sank, in what seemed to be slow motion, back into the green shallow water. I shrugged and took another bite of my bait-shop honeybun, while Fred stood there with his eyes bulging, holding my line, which was now blowing gently in the humid wind.

Months later, Fred landed the old bass, and what follows is Fred's tribute to a fine and noble fighter.

4 teaspoons ground thyme	2 garlic cloves, minced
4 teaspoons ground oregano	½ cup canola oil
4 teaspoons paprika	8 small bass, 1 pound each, skinned and cleaned; or 1 large bass, 14 pounds, skinned and cleaned
4 teaspoons cayenne pepper	
4 teaspoons salt	

Mix the first five ingredients and set aside. Rub each fish with 1 table-spoon of oil and about 1 tablespoon of the seasoning mix. Wrap the fish individually in foil, and refrigerate until ready to grill. This may be done up to 4 hours ahead of time.

Place about 1 cup of mesquite or hickory chips in a bowl and cover with water. Soak for 1 hour. Make a fire in a barbecue grill with a lid, using 5 pounds of charcoal. Let the coals burn for about 30 minutes or until you can hold your palm over the coals for 3 seconds. Set the tempera-ture on a gas grill at 375 degrees. Sprinkle the soaked wood chips over the coals or add to gas grill according to manufacturer's directions at this point, if desired.

Place the foil-wrapped fish on the grid and close the cover. Cook for 10 to 15 minutes for small fish and 25 to 30 minutes for large fish, or until the fish is flaky and opaque. Serve with lemon wedges.

Serves 8

BOILED CRAWFISH

Crawfish season brings with it cherished rituals of cooking and celebration. Big washtubs of boiling water and spices are tended by backyard cooks bent on finishing a keg of beer. At the precise moment, the teeming crustaceans are dumped into a fatal but tasty broth. To the pot are added new potatoes and corn, which soak up the wild spices and add substance to the meal. Since only the tiny yet succulent tail is edible, the crawfish are mounded on newspapers and eaten by the pound. (Ten pounds of whole crawfish yield 1 pound of cleaned tails.)

50	*pounds live crawfish*	**10**	*gallons water*
10	*lemons, cut in half*		*(approximately)*
6	*large onions, cut in half*	**5**	*pounds new potatoes,*
5	*garlic cloves*		*scrubbed*
8	*ounces liquid crab boil*	**1**	*dozen ears fresh corn,*
2	*tablespoons cayenne*		*shucked and broken in*
	pepper		*half*
2	*pounds salt*		

Place the crawfish in a large tub and wash with cool water at least twice. Remove any dead crawfish.

In a 30-gallon pot, place the lemons, onions, garlic, crab boil, pepper, salt, and water. Bring to a boil over high heat (usually maintained by a butane crawfish burner), add the potatoes and corn, and continue to boil rapidly for 15 minutes. Add the crawfish, bring back to a boil, and cook for 8 minutes. Turn off the fire and let steam for 15 minutes. Drain and serve hot or cold.

Serves 8 to 10

Featherweight Poultry and the Lighter Side of Beef

FRESH, very young chickens and home-grown prime rib were the official meats at my great-grandmother's fancy family dinners. Mama Lady's table stretched vast, covered with white damask and crammed with two or three roasts, platters of crisp-fried, delicate broilers, a dozen relishes and vegetables, hot buttered biscuits, steaming corn bread, always chess pie, wild plum jelly cake, fresh dewberries and figs, and a big pitcher of fresh cream—and yet Mama Lady would moan that she had nothing in the house.

She was a large and joyous woman with a passion for hugeness in everything surrounding her—her house, her garden, her Buick, and her own family. You never knew how many children she would have at the table besides her own and their cousins. Her house was always crowded with the neighbors' children and the neighbors themselves, as well as any children of sharecroppers and field hands. I grew up thinking that I had many more great-aunts and -uncles than I actually had.

Most husbands doubtless would have thought it impractical not only to house and feed so many extra folks but also to feed them with the youngest of spring chickens and the best part of his well-tended herd. However, my great-grandfather knew the consequences of denying Mama Lady the succulent birds and choice cuts of beef: She always wore the key to the liquor cabinet hanging on a silver chain around her wrist.

**Flank Steak with
Vegetable Marinade**

**Smoked Chicken
with Honey Marinade**

Pepper Pot Roast

**Grilled Turkey Breast
with Fresh Tomato Sauce**

**Beef Tenderloin
with Black Pepper**

Oven-Fried Chicken

Barbecued Cornish Hen

**Beef Tenderloin with
Wild Mississippi
Mushroom Sauce**

**Steaks Cooked
General Sherman's Way**

Chicken Pot Pie

**Smoked Eye of
Round Roast**

After all, what was a little extra chicken fat compared to good bourbon?

After my great-grandmother moved to town, she gave up raising chickens in the backyard, but we always had a cow in the freezer, fresh from the farm. Chicken and beef are a given in most American diets and are usually cooked in an ordinary and wholesome way, but Southerners have a penchant for overdoing everything from old roosters to beef tenderloin, their flavor hidden under a coat of coarse crumbs, further permeated by cooking oil, in a technique called "chicken-frying." In this chapter, I have grilled most of the beef and freed the poultry of the fat-clenching skin, creating healthful alternatives to our traditional flouring, frying, and smothering.

FLANK STEAK WITH VEGETABLE MARINADE

Flank steak is one of the most flavorful cuts of beef, but it has a tendency to be tough. Marinating is mandatory and slicing it thinly on the diagonal across the grain will also tenderize it. Serve this hot with the sauce or make cold sandwiches using the cooled sauce as an alternative to mayonnaise.

1 cup chopped onion	2 teaspoons fresh thyme leaves
1 cup chopped green onion tops	2 teaspoons fresh oregano leaves
1 cup chopped celery	2 teaspoons minced garlic
1 cup chopped fresh parsley	1 cup lemon juice
2 cups chopped peeled fresh tomatoes	½ cup canola oil
1 teaspoon freshly ground black pepper	2 flank steaks, 1 pound each
	½ cup dry red wine

Mix all the ingredients except the flank steak and wine and set aside. Pierce the steaks in several places on both sides with a sharp fork. Spread half the vegetable mixture in a shallow glass or ceramic dish large enough to hold both steaks and place the steaks in the marinade. Cover the steaks with the remaining marinade. Cover the dish and refrigerate for at least 6 hours, turning every now and then.

Remove the steaks from the refrigerator and let them to come to room temperature. Build a fire in a barbecue grill with 5 pounds of charcoal and burn the coals for about 30 minutes or until you can hold your palm over them for 1 to 2 seconds. Set your gas grill for 450 degrees.

Meanwhile, drain the steaks and reserve the marinade. Place the marinade in a small saucepan and simmer on low heat for 20 minutes. Add the wine and simmer for another 20 minutes. Keep warm.

Grill the steaks over hot coals for 5 minutes per side. Carve the steak across the grain diagonally into slices about ¼ inch thick. Serve the warm marinade over the sliced meat.

Serves 8

SMOKED CHICKEN WITH HONEY MARINADE

~~~~~~~~~~~~~~~~~

My favorite way to cook chicken is to roast it unstuffed. This renders a juicy and succulent bird. Slow cooking over a closed-cover grill will create the same effect and most of the fat drips away, creating an aromatic smoke.

4 tablespoons low-sodium soy sauce	**1** teaspoon dried sage
4 tablespoons honey	**½** teaspoon cayenne pepper
4 tablespoons Creole or grainy mustard	**2** teaspoon freshly ground black pepper
2 tablespoon red wine vinegar	**2** 3-pound chickens
	Canola oil, for grill

With a wire whisk, mix all the ingredients except the chicken and oil in a small bowl.

Carefully separate the chicken skin from the meat (leaving the skin still attached) by sliding your hand slowly between the skin and meat. Rub the marinade under the skin as far down on the legs as you can manage without tearing the skin. Cover the outside of the skin with the marinade, wrap in plastic wrap, and refrigerate the bird overnight.

The next day, soak 1 cup pecan or hickory chips in 2 cups water for 1 hour. Let the chicken come to room temperature. Make a fire in a barbecue grill with a cover, using 5 pounds of charcoal, and burn the coals for 30 to 40 minutes or until ash-white. When you can hold your palm over the coals for 5 seconds the fire is ready for cooking.

Sprinkle the soaked chips over the coals and close the cover for 10 minutes to allow the smoke to accumulate. If using a gas grill, set the temperature for 375 degrees or medium and place the soaked chips in a pan on the back of the grid.

Coat the grid lightly with canola oil. Insert a meat thermometer in the thickest part of the chicken thigh without touching the bone. Place the chicken, breast side up, directly on the grid about 6 inches from the coals. Close the cover. Cook for 1½ to 2 hours, until the thermometer registers 190 degrees.

Serves 8

PEPPER POT ROAST

The red and green bell peppers impart a wonderful flavor to the meat and natural gravy in this dish. Like most pot roasts, this can be refrigerated for several days and reheated often.

1 3-pound rump roast	2 large green bell peppers, cut into strips
3 garlic cloves, cut into slivers	3 large onions, sliced
2 teaspoons freshly ground black pepper	1 cup dry red wine
1 tablespoon canola oil	¼ cup low-sodium soy sauce
4 large red bell peppers, cut into strips	16 small new potatoes, washed and cut in half

Let the roast come to room temperature. Make several deep slits in one side of the roast with a sharp knife and insert the garlic slivers. Dust the roast on all sides with black pepper.

Heat the oil in a large Dutch oven over medium-high heat. Brown the roast on all sides in the hot oil. This should take about 10 minutes. Remove the roast and discard the oil.

Place the roast and the remaining ingredients except the potatoes in the Dutch oven and bring to a bubbling simmer over medium-low heat, cover, and cook slowly for 3½ hours. Keep the mixture barely bubbling.

After 3 hours, drop in the new potatoes and continue to cook for 30 minutes.

Serves 8

Note: After the roast is removed from the pot, the meat juices may be thickened by reducing the liquid by half over high heat, whisking in ¼ cup Dry Roux (page 24), and simmering over medium-high heat for 10 minutes.

GRILLED TURKEY BREAST WITH FRESH TOMATO SAUCE

I suppose back in 1682 the big old American turkey must have made quite an impression on all of those hungry Pilgrims. Quite frankly, one roasted turkey a year is all I can stand. The left-over carcass takes up residence in my refrigerator like the guest who won't leave. I finally end up boiling the skeleton and making an endless batch of turkey broth that takes up residence in my *freezer*—and I'm still left with all those bones.

A boneless, skinless turkey breast or turkey tenderloin is the answer to all my Thanksgiving prayers. Not only is this the best part of the turkey, but it lasts just long enough for one meal.

2 *garlic cloves, smashed*
3 *tablespoons apple cider vinegar*
3 *tablespoons olive oil*
1 *teaspoon fresh thyme leaves*
3 *tablespoons fresh lime juice*

1 *tablespoon low-sodium soy sauce*
1 *2½- to 3-pound boneless, skinless turkey breast*
Canola oil, for grill

Combine all the ingredients except the turkey breast and Canola oil and set aside. Pound the turkey breast to an even thickness of about 1½ inches. Place the breast in a shallow pan and add the marinade. Refrigerate for at least 3 hours, turning occasionally.

Light a fire in your barbecue grill with 5 pounds of charcoal. Burn the coals for about 30 minutes or until you can hold your palm over them for 1 to 2 seconds. Set gas grill for 375 degrees. Oil the grid lightly.

Allow the turkey to come to room temperature. Drain and reserve the liquid for basting. Place the turkey on the grid about 6 inches from the hot coals. Grill the breast, basting often, for 5 minutes on each side or until juices run clear when breast is pierced. Slice against the grain in ¼-inch slices and serve with Fresh Tomato Sauce (recipe follows).

Serves 8

Note: I like this just as well plain or with a good mustard.

FRESH TOMATO SAUCE

1 tablespoon olive oil
4 tablespoons chopped
  green onions
4 tablespoons chopped
  yellow bell pepper
1 garlic clove, minced
½ teaspoon fresh thyme
  leaves

2 cups chopped peeled
  fresh tomatoes
2 teaspoons capers
  (optional)
¼ teaspoon freshly ground
  black pepper
Salt to taste (optional)

Heat the olive oil in a small saucepan over medium-high heat and add the green onions, bell pepper, and garlic. Sauté for 7 minutes, then add the thyme and tomatoes and simmer, bubbling, for about 15 minutes. Stir in the capers, bell pepper, and salt (if desired).

Makes about 1½ cups

BEEF TENDERLOIN WITH BLACK PEPPER

I think the less you do to a beef filet, the better it tastes.

1 5-pound beef filet
1 tablespoon freshly
  ground black pepper

Canola oil, for grilling

Bring beef to room temperature. Light a fire in a barbecue grill with a lid, using 5 pounds of charcoal. Burn the coals for about 35 minutes, or until you can hold your palm over them for 3 to 4 seconds. Set the temperature on a gas grill at 350 degrees.

Rub the black pepper well into all sides of the filet. Insert meat thermometer. Brush the grid lightly with canola oil and position it about 8 inches from the heat. Place the tenderloin on the grid and close the cover. Roast for 30 minutes, turning often until the meat thermometer registers 140 degrees for rare, or to desired doneness.

Serves 8

OVEN-FRIED CHICKEN

~~~~~~~~~~~~~~~~~~~~~~~~~

Gnawing on a fried chicken leg is as natural to any Southern belle as flirting with her Daddy or calling everyone "honey" and "sugar plum." Since fried chicken is eaten with great abandon and quite often, this low-fat version is necessary to those of us who want to fit into last year's pantelettes.

2 *3-pound chickens, cut up for frying*	**1** *whole egg plus 3 egg whites*
1 *cup all-purpose flour*	**1** *tablespoon Tabasco*
2 *tablespoons plus 1 teaspoon salt*	**2** *cups toasted bread crumbs*
2 *tablespoons freshly ground black pepper*	**1** *teaspoon ground white pepper*
3 *teaspoons ground thyme*	**2** *teaspoons paprika*
1 *cup milk*	

Cover a baking sheet with wax paper and set aside.

Remove the skin and scrape off any visible fat from the chicken pieces. In a large bowl, mix the flour, 2 tablespoons salt, black pepper, and 2 teaspoons of the thyme. Set aside.

In a separate bowl, beat together the milk, egg, egg white, and Tabasco. Set aside. Mix the bread crumbs, white pepper, paprika, and remaining salt and thyme in another bowl and set aside.

Roll the chicken pieces in the flour, dip in the egg wash, and roll in the bread crumb mixture. Place the chicken on the wax paper, cover with plastic wrap, and refrigerate for 1 hour.

Preheat the oven to 350 degrees.

Place the chicken on a footed grid or rack. Put the rack in a shallow baking dish and place in the oven. Bake for 45 minutes or until the juices run clear when chicken is pierced.

Serves 6 to 8

BARBECUED CORNISH HEN

These little hens are a new twist on that old favorite, barbecued chicken.

8 large Cornish hens
4 cups applesauce
2 cups frozen apple juice concentrate, thawed
½ cup lemon juice
1 cup tomato paste
½ cup honey
1 teaspoon salt
1 teaspoon ground white pepper
2 teaspoons ground ginger
3 large garlic cloves, minced
Canola oil, for grilling

Cut the hens in half by inserting a knife in the lower side of the cavity and cutting down either side of the backbone. Discard the backbone. Flip the hens over and cut vertically down the center of the breast. Remove the skin. Place the hens in a large dish. Combine the rest of the ingredients except the canola oil and pour over the hens. Marinate for at least 3 hours.

Build a fire in a barbecue grill with 5 pounds of charcoal. Burn the coals for about 30 minutes or until you can hold your palm over them for 3 to 4 seconds. If you have a gas grill, set the heat at 375 degrees.

Coat the grid with canola oil. Place the hens on the grid about 6 inches from the coals. Grill for 15 minutes on each side, basting with the marinade until the juices run clear when hens are pierced with a fork.

Serves 8

BEEF TENDERLOIN WITH WILD MISSISSIPPI MUSHROOM SAUCE

Edible mushrooms grow wild in the moist and mossy woods close to my home. I have a trusted friend who can tell these tasty fungi apart from their botanical cousins. If you don't have such a pal, I suggest that you use the shitake or porcini varieties found in the produce section of your local market or specialty foods store.

- **3** cups chopped wild mushrooms
- **1** medium yellow onion, sliced
- **1** beef tenderloin (3 to 4 pounds), fat trimmed
- **2** tablespoons extra virgin olive oil
- **¼** cup finely chopped green onions
- **¼** cup chopped red bell pepper
- **1** teaspoon fresh thyme leaves
  Salt and freshly ground black pepper to taste
- **¼** cup water
- **¼** cup red wine
- **1** tablespoon of margarine, if desired

Preheat the oven to 425 degrees.

Spread 1 cup of the mushrooms and the onion slices in the bottom of a shallow baking pan and set aside.

Using a sharp knife, make a cut lengthwise down the center of the tenderlion through two-thirds of the thickness. Spread open the meat and pound slightly with a mallet.

Heat one tablespoon of the oil in a skillet over medium heat. Add the green onions and sauté for 5 minutes. Add the remaining mushrooms, bell pepper, and thyme, and sauté for about 10 minutes or until the mushrooms are tender. Add salt and pepper to taste.

Spread the mushroom mixture over the open tenderloin. Form the tenderloin into its original shape and tie closed in several places. Rub the surface of the beef with remaining oil and sprinkle with freshly ground black pepper. Place seam side down on the prepared bed of mushrooms and onions.

Roast for 45 minutes for medium rare, or until described doneness. If the beef begins to look scorched as it cooks, add the water to the pan.

Remove the roast to a warm serving platter. Place the baking pan over medium heat and deglaze the pan with the wine. Swirl in a little margarine, if desired.

Slice the meat, spoon the mushroom sauce over it and serve with wild rice or grits, or perhaps popovers.

Serves 8

STEAKS COOKED GENERAL SHERMAN'S WAY

This recipe came to me from my cousin Barbara Ruth, an avid barbecue cook and local expert. She is one of the few people who has the same untamed enthusiasm for food and its endless possibilities as I do. This is one of her favorite recipes. You'll taste why.

8 *rib-eye steaks (1¼ inches thick), trimmed of fat from the outside*
2 *teaspoons minced garlic*

4 *teaspoons freshly ground black pepper*
1 *pint decent bourbon*

Pierce each steak through in several places with an ice pick. Rub each with ¼ teaspoon garlic and ½ teaspoon black pepper. Place the steaks in a shallow pan and pour the bourbon over. Cover, place in the refrigerator, and marinate for at least 3 hours, turning often.

Build a fire in a barbecue grill with 5 pounds of charcoal. Burn the coals for about 30 minutes or until you can hold your palm over them for 1 to 2 seconds; the fire should be very hot. Set the temperature on a gas grill for 450 degrees.

Place the grid fairly close to the coals—about 6 inches—and place the cold steaks on the grid directly over the hot coals. Grill the steaks for 4 minutes on each side. As the bourbon drips into the hot coals, the fire will flame just like Atlanta.

Serves 8

Note: These steaks will be "blackened" on the outside and rare in the middle.

CHICKEN POT PIE

There is nothing that smells more like a loving meal than a chicken pot pie. This recipe stretches that well-fed feeling by adding more vegetables and eliminating the egg yolks and butter. Both the filling and the crust may be made two days ahead and stored in the refrigerator until ready to assemble and bake.

Crust

3 *cups all-purpose flour*
1 *teaspoon salt*
1 *cup plus two tablespoons (2¼ sticks) chilled margarine*

6 *to 10 tablespoons ice water*

Filling

1 *tablespoon margarine*
1 *cup chopped onion*
1 *cup chopped celery*
1 *cup diced carrots*
2 *cups sliced mushrooms*
2 *cups chopped peeled fresh tomatoes*
2 *cups chopped broccoli*
2 *tablespoons chopped fresh basil*

2 *cups chopped chicken breast meat, trimmed of all skin and fat*
2 *tablespoons cornstarch*
1 *cup Defatted Chicken Stock (page 20) Salt and freshly ground black pepper to taste*

To make the crust, mix the flour and salt in a large bowl with a fork. With two knives or a pastry cutter, cut the margarine into the flour mixture in small pieces until the dough resembles coarse meal. Add the water and work it in with a fork until you have a smooth dough. Gather the dough into a ball and refrigerate for 30 minutes. This makes enough dough for 1 large deep-dish pie or 2 regular pies.

Preheat the oven to 400 degrees.

To make the filling, heat the margarine in a large skillet over medium heat. Add the onion, celery, and carrots, and sauté for 15 minutes. Add the mushrooms, tomatoes, broccoli, basil, and chicken, and cook, stirring, for 10 minutes.

Dissolve the cornstarch in the stock and stir into the vegetable mixture. Cook for 5 minutes until thickened. Add salt and pepper to taste. Remove the skillet from the heat and spoon the mixture into a 10 x 2½-inch casserole. Set aside.

Place the chilled dough on a lightly floured surface and roll it out to fit your casserole. Cover the filling with the dough, pinching the edges all the way around. Make some air holes in the crust and bake for 30 minutes or until the crust is nicely browned.

Serves 8

SMOKED EYE OF ROUND ROAST

An eye of round roast is a lean cut of beef that responds beautifully to a tenderizing marinade.

1 *3- to 4-pound eye of round beef roast*	**2** *tablespoons Creole mustard or grainy mustard*
3 *tablespoons low-sodium soy sauce*	**2** *tablespoons canola oil*
3 *tablespoons Worcestershire sauce*	**1** *tablespoon freshly ground black pepper*

Place the roast in a shallow pan. Mix the remaining ingredients and pour over the roast, turning to coat well. Refrigerate overnight.

The next day, bring roast to room temperature. Soak 1 cup hickory chips or, for a more delicate flavor, pecan chips in 2 cups water. Build a fire in a barbecue grill with a cover, using 5 or 10 pounds of charcoal, depending on its size. Burn the coals for 35 to 40 minutes or until you can hold your palm over them for 4 or 5 seconds and the coals are ash-white. Set the temperature on a gas grill for 325 degrees. Sprinkle the wet chips over the hot coals or add to gas grill according to manufacturer's directions. Close the lid for 10 minutes to allow the smoke to accumulate.

Place a meat thermometer in the center of the roast. Place the roast on the grid about 6 inches from the coals and close the lid. Cover and cook for 30 minutes or until the meat thermometer registers 150 for rare; cook 10 minutes longer for medium.

Serves 8

Eatin' **High on the Hog**

D O W N South, to say that someone is eating high on the hog is to imply that they are living in a luxurious manner. I suppose this comes from the physical locations of the better cuts of meat, such as the tenderloin, and their close proximity to the top of the pig. Considering that one of the most common sights in Southern convenience stores is a three-foot-high jar filled with pickled pigs' feet (a bargain to be sure), this saying makes plenty of sense.

Apricot Spare Ribs

Spicy Smoked Pork Tenderloin

Plum-Stuffed Pork Loin with Fresh Plum Sauce

This chapter takes advantage of the better cuts of pork such as pork tenderloins and center-cut pork chops. These cuts have very little fat and require a shorter cooking time than traditionally practiced for pork as a whole. The days of selecting a fat piece of pork that would remain juicy over the prolonged cooking time are over. This method of overcooking pork came from fear of trichinosis. To put your worries aside, it was established long ago that trichinae are killed when the meat reaches an internal temperature of 137 degrees. I know that most people will not eat a medium-rare piece of pork, so I stick to the standard of 160 degrees or until the juices run clear. This will keep the meat tender, juicy, and safe.

Grilled Honey and Mustard Pork Tenderloin

Low-Fat Sausages

Ham Stuffed with Crawfish Tails

Butterflied Pork Chops with Apple Marinade

Stuffed Spiced Crown Roast of Pork

Pork Chops with Hot Pepper Jelly

APRICOT SPARE RIBS

The barbecue pit, or grill, is an integral fixture in backyards all over the Deep South, and from Florida to Texas, the bigger the pit the better. Enthusiastic barbecue cooks design and build their own pits, which look like rolling, smoking, metal coffins on stilts. Most pits can smoke a hefty pig on one end while grilling hamburgers on the other and warming bread in the middle.

Most cookouts are really cookoffs for show-offs. We labor over our tubular furnaces all day, basting, turning, and fanning until each meat reaches its smoky perfection. Around twilight the table is set and every cook carves the fruit of his or her labor for the lucky bunch to enjoy.

This recipe calls for parboiling the ribs before grilling, which not only saves time at the cookout but also renders most of the fat from those hard-to-trim places.

1 cup fresh apricot puree	¼ teaspoon ground cumin
3 tablespoons apple cider vinegar	Scant ¼ teaspoon grated nutmeg
3 tablespoons low-sodium soy sauce	1 garlic clove, roasted (see Note, page 77), peeled, and minced
2 tablespoons Worcestershire sauce	1 cup Oven-Browned Onions (page 152)
3 tablespoons canola oil	4 pounds pork spare ribs, well trimmed of visible fat
3 tablespoons molasses	
¼ teaspoon cayenne pepper	
½ teaspoon ground thyme	1 teaspoon salt

Mix all of the ingredients except the ribs and salt and set aside. Place the ribs in a large kettle, cover with water, and add the salt. Bring to a simmer, cover, and cook for 30 minutes. Drain the ribs on paper towels and place them in a large bowl. Pour the sauce over the ribs and marinate for at least 2 hours.

Cover 1 cup of your favorite wood chips with water and soak for 1 hour. Meanwhile, light the charcoal in a grill with a cover and burn the coals for about 35 minutes, or until ash-gray and you can hold your hand over the coals for 3 seconds. Set the temperature on a gas grill for 375 degrees. Sprinkle the presoaked chips directly onto the charcoal or add to gas grill according to manufacturer's directions. Close the cover to distribute the heat evenly and allow the smoke to accumulate.

Brush the grid with oil. Place the ribs on the grid 6 inches over the coals and grill, with the cover closed, for 15 minutes on each side or until crisp. Baste often with the sauce. Serve hot.

Serves 6 to 8

SPICY SMOKED PORK TENDERLOIN

~~~~~~~~~~~~~~~~~~~~~

This is so good it's a miracle that the pork ever makes it all the way to the table, much less to someone else's plate. I recommend limiting yourself to one "tasting" while slicing this dish. Try serving this on canapés at your next party with different condiments such as chutney and homemade catsup.

2 *teaspoons ground cumin*	**2** *pork tenderloins, about*
1 *teaspoon ground thyme*	*¾ pound each*
½ teaspoon grated nutmeg	*½ cup low-sodium soy*
2 *teaspoons freshly*	*sauce*
ground black pepper	

Mix the cumin, thyme, nutmeg, and pepper and rub into all sides of the tenderloins. Wrap in plastic and refrigerate overnight.

Soak 1 cup of wood chips in 2 cups of water for 1 hour. Meanwhile, build a fire in a lidded barbecue grill using 5 pounds of charcoal. Allow the coals to burn for 30 minutes or until you can hold your palm over them for 5 seconds. Preheat a gas grill to 450 degrees. Scatter the soaked chips over the coals and close the lid for 10 minutes.

Insert a meat thermometer into one of the tenderloins. Place the tenderloins on the grid directly over the coals and baste with soy sauce. Close the lid and cook for 15 minutes. Turn the tenderloins and baste with soy sauce again. Close the lid and cook for another 10 to 15 minutes or until the meat thermometer registers 160 degrees. The meat should be slightly pink in the center and quite moist. Serve hot or cold.

Serves 8

Plum-Stuffed Pork Loin with Fresh Plum Sauce

~~~~~~~~~~~~~~~~~~~~~~~~~~

Although the word *delicate* is rarely associated with pork, in this case it applies. Fresh lean pork loin can be quite juicy and gentle to the palate as well as nutritious. The fresh thyme and tart plums flavor this roast throughout, in a gentle way not at all reminiscent of the usual outdoor barbecued pork.

1 *3-pound boned pork roast, split in half by your butcher*

Stuffing

½ *cup pitted fresh plums (about about 3 medium plums)*
2 *tablespoons minced fresh thyme leaves*

¼ *cup chopped fresh pineapple*
Pinch of freshly ground black pepper

Glaze

½ *cup low-sugar plum jam*
½ *teaspoon lemon juice*
1 *teaspoon freshly ground black pepper*

¼ *teaspoon ground ginger*
¼ *teaspoon salt*

Prepare the grill as for the Grilled Honey and Mustard Pork Tenderloin recipe (page 110).

Trim the roast of all visible fat. Mix all the ingredients for the stuffing and spread on the cut side of the pork roast. Fold the other half over and truss the roast with twine. Insert meat thermometer. Set aside.

Mix the ingredients for the glaze in a small saucepan and heat on low until the jam is melted, about 10 minutes. Brush the roast all over with the glaze, then place roast on the grid. Cover and roast for about 2 hours or until the meat thermometer registers 160 degrees. Baste often.

The "stuffing" will be absorbed into the pork, essentially basting the meat from the inside. Serve with Fresh Plum Sauce (recipe follows).

Serves 8 to 10

Note: This may be prepared in a conventional oven. Sear the meat in a 450 degree oven for 15 minutes, brush with more glaze, cover with foil, lower the heat to 325 degrees, and roast for 1 hour and 45 minutes, or until a meat thermometer registers 160 degrees. Serve hot or cold.

FRESH PLUM SAUCE

1½ *pounds tart plums, cut in half and pitted*
¼ *cup water*
1 *garlic clove*
½ *teaspoon fresh thyme leaves*

Pinch of ground cloves
Pinch of cayenne pepper
½ *teaspoon salt*
¼ *cup sugar*

Place the plums and water in a saucepan over medium-high heat and cook for 20 minutes until the plums are soft. Drain, save the liquid, and put the solids through a food mill or rub through a fine sieve.

Return the liquid and the pulp to the saucepan. Add the remaining ingredients to the saucepan and simmer over low heat for 30 minutes or until thick.

Makes about 1½ cups

GRILLED HONEY AND MUSTARD PORK TENDERLOIN

~~~~~~~~~~~~~~~~~~~~~~~~

Pork tenderloin is a lean, solid meat cut from the center and sirloin portions of the loin. Although a superior cut of meat, it is fairly inexpensive, and perfect for grilling.

2 *cups buttermilk*
8 *garlic cloves, crushed*
2 *tablespoons Tabasco*
2 *pork tenderloins, about ³/₄ pound each*

4 *tablespoons Creole mustard*
4 *tablespoons honey*
4 *tablespoons low-sodium soy sauce*

Mix the buttermilk, garlic, and Tabasco in a bowl and pour over the pork tenderloins. Cover and refrigerate for at least 6 hours.

Soak 1 cup of hickory or pecan wood chips in 2 cups of water for at least 1 hour before heating the grill.

Light the charcoal in a grill with a cover and burn the coals, uncovered, until they turn ash-gray, about 30 to 40 minutes. (If you can hold your hand over the coals for 5 seconds they are ready for covered cooking.) Add the presoaked chips to the coals, then close the cover to allow the heat to distribute evenly and the smoke to accumulate. If you have a gas grill, turn the dial to 400 degrees and add the presoaked chips, according to manufacturer's directions, after about 10 minutes. Cover the lid for about 10 minutes before adding the meat.

Mix the mustard, honey, and soy sauce. Drain the tenderloins and pat dry. Insert meat thermometer. Brush the meat all over with the mustard mixture and place in the middle of the grid, directly over the coals. Close the cover and smoke for 15 minutes. Turn and baste the tenderloins. Close the cover and smoke for another 15 minutes or until a meat thermometer registers 160 degrees and the juices run clear. Slice thinly and serve hot or cold.

Serves 8

LOW-FAT SAUSAGES

~~~~~~~~~~~~~~~~~~~~~~~~~~~~

If you want to test the flavor while adding the spices, simply cook a bite-size piece of the sausage mixture, taste it, then adjust the seasoning.

2 *pounds lean ground pork (well-trimmed loin)*
1 *pound ground turkey ham*
¼ *teaspoon cayenne pepper*
¼ *teaspoon dried sage*
¼ *teaspoon dried thyme*
¼ *teaspoon ground cumin*
¼ *teaspoon grated nutmeg*

⅛ *teaspoon ground cinnamon*
⅛ *teaspoon ground cloves*
1 *teaspoon light brown sugar (optional)*
½ *teaspoon freshly ground black pepper*
1 *garlic clove, minced (optional)*

Place all the ingredients in a large bowl and mix with your hands, lifting not mashing. If you overwork this it will become tough. Wrap and refrigerate for 12 hours.

Form mixture into patties and "fry" in a nonstick skillet for about 10 minutes, until nicely browned on both sides.

Makes about 1 dozen patties

Note: Since this sausage contains very little fat, it will not turn dark brown when cooked but, rather, will be flecked with brown. You can also stuff the sausage into casings, if you prefer. (Sausages in casings are wonderful on the grill.)

HAM STUFFED WITH CRAWFISH TAILS

~~~~~~~~~~~~~~~~~~~~

When selecting your ham for this recipe, ask your butcher for assistance. You want to select a lean ham with a reasonably low amount of salt and one that will hold its shape after the bone is removed. Have your butcher debone the ham, then remove the shank end and all of the visible fat. When you get it home, go back over the ham to trim any fat the butcher might have missed, especially around the bone cavity.

This is a rich springtime dish and should be accompanied by a very light spring vegetable such as steamed squash or green beans with rosemary.

1 tablespoon canola oil
½ cup chopped onion
½ cup chopped green bell pepper
½ cup chopped celery
1 pound Boiled Crawfish tails (page 85), with fat
¼ teaspoon ground thyme
2 bay leaves
¼ teaspoon cayenne pepper
Scant ¼ teaspoon salt

1 teaspoon Worcestershire sauce
1 tablespoon lemon juice
1 cup cooked rice, cooked in Defatted Chicken Stock (page 20)
1 5-pound smoked ham, bone and shank end removed, trimmed of all but a thin layer of outer fat and scored
1 large onion, sliced
½ cup water

Glaze

1 tablespoon Dijon-style mustard
1 tablespoon dry white wine

¼ teaspoon ground thyme

Heat the oil in a large skillet over medium-high heat and sauté the onion, pepper, and celery for 20 minutes, until soft and lightly browned. Turn the heat to medium-low and add the crawfish with fat, thyme, bay leaves, cayenne pepper, salt, Worcestershire sauce, and lemon juice. Stir over medium-low heat for 15 minutes. Add the rice and fluff with a fork.

Preheat the oven to 350 degrees.

Spread the rice mixture generously in the ham cavity, reshape the ham, and truss tightly. (Any leftover stuffing can be saved, reheated, and eaten for lunch with a green salad.) Place the ham in a roasting pan on a bed of sliced onion and pour in the water. Cover with foil. Bake the ham for 20 minutes, remove the foil, whisk together glaze ingredients, and pour over the ham, and bake for another 25 to 30 minutes or until nicely browned. Serve immediately.

Serves 10 to 12

BUTTERFLIED PORK CHOPS WITH APPLE MARINADE

This dish makes fast work of supper if you marinate the chops in the morning.

1 *cup frozen apple juice concentrate, thawed*

½ *cup low-sodium soy sauce*

2½ *tablespoons Creole mustard*

2 *tablespoons chopped fresh basil*

4 *garlic cloves, minced*

8 *½-inch-thick center-cut pork chops, boned, butterflied, and trimmed of all visible fat.*

Whisk together the first 5 ingredients and pour over the chops in a flat container large enough to hold the chops in one layer. Cover and marinate the chops in the refrigerator for at least 6 hours.

Preheat the broiler.

Bring the chops to room temperature. Spray a broiling pan with non-stick vegetable coating, then place the chops in the pan. Broil about 3 inches from the heat for 7½ minutes on each side. Baste with marinade.

Serves 8

STUFFED SPICED CROWN
ROAST OF PORK

~~~~~~~~~~~~~~~~~~~~

When selecting this roast, look for a lean one and have the butcher trim it of all visible fat. Roasting it on the rack allows the remaining fat to drip away from the meat.

This is a fairly easy yet delicious and impressive holiday entrée.

Crown roast of pork, well trimmed, about 7 pounds
½ teaspoon salt
½ teaspoon freshly ground black pepper, or to taste
½ teaspoon ground thyme
¼ teaspoon mace
½ teaspoon ground cumin
1½ cups cooked long grain rice, cooked in Defatted Chicken Stock (page 20)

½ cup cooked wild rice
½ cup cooked black-eyed peas
½ cup chopped green onions
½ cup toasted chopped pecans
½ cup chopped green bell pepper
½ cup chopped red bell pepper
Salt to taste

Preheat the oven to 325 degrees.

Cover a rack large enough to hold the roast with aluminum foil and place it in your roasting pan. Rub the roast inside and out with the salt, ½ teaspoon pepper, thyme, mace, and cumin. Place the roast, bone ends up, on the rack and bake for 1 hour.

Toss together the rest of the ingredients and season to taste.

Remove the roast from the oven and cover the rib ends with foil. Spoon the rice mixture into the roast and cover with foil. Insert a meat thermometer into the roast without touching the bone. Bake for 1½ more hours or until the thermometer reaches 160 degrees. Remove the foil and let the roast stand for about 15 minutes before serving.

Serves 12

PORK CHOPS WITH HOT PEPPER JELLY

~~~~~~~~~~~~~~~~~~~~~~~~~~~~~~~~~

Hot pepper jelly is a staple in my kitchen and has been made in Natchez for as long as anyone can remember. It's good on game, poultry, and cheese, in addition to pork. Hot pepper jelly may be ordered from Lee Bailey's aunt, Freddy Bailey, at the Tot, Teen, and Mom Shop, 400 South Commerce Street, Natchez, MS 39120. She's made the jelly for more than forty years.

8 *1-inch-thick loin pork chops, butterflied*

½ *cup hot red pepper jelly (not green pepper jelly)*

Trim the chops of all visible fat and set aside.

Preheat the broiler or heat the coals in your barbecue grill until you can hold your palm over them for 3 seconds (about 30 minutes).

In a small saucepan, melt the jelly over low heat until liquid, about 5 minutes. Spread the chops with the melted jelly and grill or broil for about 7 minutes per side or until lightly browned. The chops should be a little pink in the middle.

Serves 8

Note: I love the taste of hot pepper jelly, so I serve extra on the side.

Wild **Things**

man in ex-
pensive, new, yet muddy camou-
flage hops out of an expensive,
new, yet muddy Jeep. He kicks his
shamefully muddy boots off outside and holds open the back door
with one thermal-socked foot, his
gun in one hand and his bright
orange hat in the other. His bud-

dies drag their still-feathered or -hooved bloody prizes into the spotless kitchen. They pluck and clean and skin and debone to their hearts' content, guzzling a well-earned beer or two along the way. Then they proudly slam the freshly killed meat onto the kitchen table. The woman of the house helplessly surveys the complete destruction of her kitchen, staring first at the game and then at the hunters, wondering which to hit with the meat mallet first.

While this is a typical image in the South, it has been my experience that most men or women who bag lots of game also cook their fair share, and are as proud of their recipes as they are of their Jeeps and guns—or spotless kitchens. These hunters are not only enthusiastic about a day in the woods but full of experimental recipes, which they are eager to share with fellow cooks.

If you are lucky like me, you have generous friends who will both share their cooking secrets and give you part of their fall haul. Make it your business to find out just how soon after the kill the carcasses were butchered; riding around with a dead deer strapped to the bumper of a Jeep on a balmy Mississippi Thanksgiving afternoon is

Grilled Wild Duck with Cranberry Glaze

Grilled Quail with Blackberry Jam

Quail Baked in Grits

Quail in Beaujolais

Smoked Quail

Oven-Barbecued Venison Hindquarter Roast

Back Strap Venison Steaks

Venison Chili

Venison Burgers

Venison Grillards

Venison Shoulder Roast

Venison Medallions with Tarragon

Venison Tenderloin

not a good method of tenderization. The sooner the beast is in the freezer or on the grill, the better it will taste. A properly field-dressed carcass will not have an offensively wild flavor that needs to be covered with an offensively fattening gravy.

In this chapter I provide recipes that eliminate the usual larding, flouring, and frying of meat, and the almost inevitable draping of bacon over every poultry breast plucked. Deer and wild birds roam and forage naturally, so they get plenty of exercise and are not pumped full of hormones. I say we should take advantage of this natural lean texture instead of trying to fatten it up.

Mounted racks and feather fantails can be proof of a successful hunt, but to celebrate with a meal is a way of sharing the achievement. Like a final step through wet November woods, a hunt dinner completes the hunter's cycle. The journey ends where it began, back in our warm homes with family and friends.

GRILLED WILD DUCK WITH CRANBERRY GLAZE

These ducks are parboiled to expedite the grilling and to tame the wild flavor. They are delicious served with Pecan Wild Rice (page 63).

8 *wild ducks, about 2 to 2½ pounds each*
2 *cups fresh cranberries*
2 *cups light brown sugar, packed*
8 *cups water*
2 *lemons, sliced*
2 *oranges, sliced*
2 *whole cloves*
1 *cinnamon stick*
Canola oil
Salt and freshly ground black pepper to taste

Insert a knife in the cavity of each duck and cut down one side of the backbone. Cut down the other side of the backbone and remove it. Flip each duck over and split it vertically down the breast. Poke the breast through the skin with a sharp fork at 1-inch intervals. Slash the fatty portion around the leg with a sharp knife. Set aside.

Combine the cranberries with the sugar in a medium saucepan over medium-high heat. Bring to a boil and reduce heat. Stirring constantly, simmer the mixture for 20 minutes or until the cranberries burst, the sugar is melted, and the mixture has thickened. Remove from heat.

Make a fire in a barbecue grill with a cover, using 5 pounds of charcoal. Burn the coals for about 30 minutes or until you can hold your hand over them for 2½ to 3 seconds. If using a gas grill, preheat to 400 degrees. About 20 minutes before the coals are ready, combine the water, lemon and orange slices, cloves, and cinnamon in a large pot and heat to boiling. Add the duck halves and simmer over medium-low heat for 15 minutes. Remove the duck halves from the pot and pat dry with paper towels. Sprinkle with salt and pepper. Brush with the glaze.

Brush the grid lightly with oil. Place the duck halves skin side up on the grid and prick all over with a fork. Spoon more sauce over the ducks, close the cover, and cook for 10 minutes. Remove the cover, baste, and flip the ducks over. Grill for about 12 more minutes or until the ducks are crisp and done.

Serves 8

GRILLED QUAIL WITH BLACKBERRY JAM

Southerners usually eat quail once a year during the traditional hunting season. Typically, they are floured and fried, then smothered with a thick gravy and served with grits. It's no wonder we reserve this rich and weighty meal for one season.

Fortunately, today's farm-raised quail are available in the grocery market year-round. These delicate birds lend themselves to all kinds of lean and tasty entrées. This light dish is perfect for a summer cookout.

16 quail, split in half lengthwise	**4** tablespoons Tabasco
1 teaspoon ground thyme	**1** cup low-sugar blackberry jam
3 cups buttermilk	Salt and freshly ground
4 garlic cloves	black pepper to taste

To split the quail, place each on its back, insert a sharp knife into the cavity, and cut along the backbone. Flip the quail over, spread out the breast skin side down, and cut the breast vertically down the center. If you're like me and would rather not have to fool with all those little-bitty bones at the table, debone the breasts, leaving the wing and leg intact.

Mix the thyme, buttermilk, garlic, and Tabasco. Place the quail in a shallow dish and pour this mixture over them. Allow the quail to marinate for 1 hour or refrigerate overnight.

Drain the birds and pat dry. Melt the jam over low heat or microwave for 1½ minutes. Spread each quail with jam on both sides. Set aside.

Build a fire in a barbecue grill with 5 pounds of charcoal. If using a gas grill, set the temperature for 425 degrees. Burn the coals for 25 to 30 minutes, or until you can hold your palm over them for only about 2½ seconds. Place the quail skin side down directly over the coals and grill for 12 minutes. Turn the birds and grill for another 12 minutes or until nicely browned on both sides. Serve immediately as an appetizer or entrée.

Serves 8

QUAIL BAKED IN GRITS

Baking the quail submerged in the grits keeps the birds moist. This eliminates the need for a fattening gravy, and imparts a rich flavor to the grits.

4 cups buttermilk
2 teaspoons Tabasco
2 teaspoons fresh thyme, or 1 teaspoon ground thyme
16 quail
5 cups Defatted Chicken Stock (page 20)
1½ cups grits
1 cup Oven-Browned Onions (page 152)

½ cup evaporated skim milk
1 egg plus 1 egg white, beaten
½ teaspoon salt
½ teaspoon freshly ground black pepper
2 green bell peppers

Mix the buttermilk, Tabasco, and thyme. Place the quail in a large bowl and pour this mixture over them. Refrigerate for at least 3 hours.

Bring the stock to the boil in a medium saucepan and stir in the grits. Reduce the heat to low and simmer the grits, covered, for about 20 minutes, or until the liquid is absorbed and a spoon leaves a deep trail. Set aside.

Preheat the broiler. Drain the quail from the seasoned buttermilk. Spray a broiler pan with nonstick vegetable coating and place the quail on the pan. Place the pan about 3 inches from the broiler and turn with tongs until nicely flecked with brown on all sides, about 2 minutes per side or 10 minutes total. Remove the pan from the oven and keep warm.

Turn the oven to 350 degrees. Beat together the grits, onions, evaporated milk, egg and egg white, salt, and pepper. Spoon this mixture into a large casserole. Place the quail close together and about 1 inch down into the grits. Cut little "breast shields" about 1 inch square from the bell peppers and place one over each quail breast. Bake the casserole uncovered for 30 to 40 minutes, or until the quail juices run clear when birds are pricked with a fork. Serve immediately.

Serves 8

QUAIL IN BEAUJOLAIS

~~~~~~~~~~~~~~~~~~~~~~~~~~~~

This dish is a meal in a bowl. The sauce will be thin but exqui-site, so you might want to add a soup spoon to the place setting. A fresh green salad and crusty French bread round out the meal nicely.

 4 *lemons, cut in half*
16 *quail*
 2 *tablespoons (¼ stick) margarine, softened*
 2 *cups sliced onions*
⅓ *cup cognac*
 3 *cups Beaujolais wine*
 2 *garlic cloves*
 2 *bay leaves, crumbled*
 1 *tablespoon chopped fresh basil*
 1 *tablespoon chopped fresh parsley*
 1 *tablespoon chopped fresh thyme*
 1 *dozen large domestic mushroom caps*
   Salt and freshly ground black pepper to taste
½ *cup Light Cracklins (page 163)*

Preheat the broiler and spray a perforated broiler pan with nonstick vegetable coating.

Squeeze the lemon halves liberally over each quail and rub each with about ½ teaspoon of the softened margarine, just enough to coat them. Place the quail fairly close together on the broiler pan and place the pan about 2½ inches from the heat. Broil the birds until flecked with brown on all sides, turning frequently, about 10 minutes. Turn off the broiler and remove the birds from the oven.

Cover the bottom of a heavy Dutch oven with the sliced onions, then arrange the quail tightly on top of the onions. Place over high heat, pour in the cognac, and ignite it. When the alcohol burns off, pour in enough wine to cover the quail halfway, and bring to a simmer. Add the garlic, bay leaves, basil, parsley, and thyme. Cover, reduce the heat to low, and keep at a gentle simmer for 1 hour. About 15 minutes before serving, drop in the mushroom caps and let them simmer in the sauce. Add salt and pepper to taste.

Serve the quail in large soup plates surrounded by onions and mush-rooms. Spoon a good amount of the sauce over the birds and top with the Light Cracklins.

Serves 8

SMOKED QUAIL

~~~~~~~~~~~~~~~

For a more aromatic smoke, try throwing fresh thyme sprigs directly onto the coals along with the wood chips.

16 *quail*
½ *cup low-sodium soy sauce*

1 *teaspoon ground thyme*

Place the quail in a large bowl. Mix the soy sauce and thyme and pour over the quail. Turn them to coat and marinate for 1 hour.

Meanwhile, soak 1 cup of hickory or your favorite wood chips in 2 cups of water for 1 hour. Make a fire in a barbecue grill with a cover, using 5 pounds of charcoal, and heat the coals until they turn ash-gray, about 45 minutes, or until you can hold your palm over the fire for 5 seconds. If using a gas grill, preheat to 325 degrees. Scatter the soaked wood chips over the coals, or add to gas grill according to manufacturer's directions. Close the cover, and allow the smoke to accumulate for 10 minutes. Place the quail breast side up on the grid, close the cover, and smoke for 30 minutes, basting occasionally with the marinade. Serve immediately.

Serves 8

OVEN-BARBECUED VENISON
HINDQUARTER ROAST

~~~~~~~~~~~~~~~~~~~~

In order to remove all of the connective tissue from the hind-quarter, once the bone is removed, I separate the roast into the sections it naturally falls into. This leaves two small chunks of meat and one large piece. I have the hunter debone and quarter this hindquarter, leaving me with four 5- to 6-pound roasts that are much easier to freeze and prepare than the whole hind-quarter.

1 *6-pound boned hindquarter roast*
1 *teaspoon minced garlic*
1 *teaspoon celery seed*
3 *tablespoons freshly ground black pepper (see Note)*
1 *teaspoon ground ginger*
4 *large bay leaves, crumbled*
1 *12-ounce can tomato paste*
1 *cup low-sodium soy sauce*
½ *cup Worcestershire sauce*
1 *cup tightly packed dark brown sugar*
2 *medium onions, sliced*

With a sharp knife, remove all the fat and connective tissue from the venison. (This tissue looks almost like plastic wrap on the surface of the meat.) Tear off 2 large pieces of foil—enough to completely enclose the meat. Place the foil in a roaster and the meat on the foil. Rub the venison on all sides with garlic. Whisk together the remaining ingredients except the onions and coat the meat with this sauce. Place the onions on top of the meat and seal the foil. You can prepare the dish ahead of time up to this point and refrigerate.

If refrigerated, allow the meat to come to room temperature. Insert a meat thermometer. Preheat the oven to 350 degrees.

Roast the meat in the foil for 2½ to 3 hours or until meat thermometer registers 175 to 180 for well done. Since venison is extremely lean, the sauce may be served directly from the roaster without any degreasing process.

Serves 8

Note: 3 tablespoons of pepper make this sauce spicy enough for me, but if your taste buds are more sensitive to heat, you may want to reduce the amount.

BACK STRAP VENISON STEAKS

Back strap resembles a beef tenderloin in size, lean texture, and, if correctly field-dressed, flavor. The most significant aspect of this recipe is the way the steaks are cut from the loin. They should be sliced on the diagonal as if slicing vegetables for Chinese cooking.

1 *3-pound venison back strap, cut into about 6 1-inch-thick steaks, about 3 to 4 ounces each*

Olive oil
Freshly ground black pepper to taste

Rub each steak with a small amount of olive oil on both sides and sprinkle with black pepper to taste.

Make a fire in your barbecue grill with 5 pounds of charcoal and burn the coals for about 30 minutes or until you can hold your palm over them for 2 to 3 seconds. If using a gas grill, set the temperature for 450 degrees. The grid should be about 6 inches from the heat. Grill the steaks for about 4 minutes on each side for rare, 5 to 6 minutes for medium. Serve hot or slice thin and serve cold on sandwiches.

Serves 6

VENISON CHILI

~~~~~~~~~~~~~~~~~~~~~~~~

My mother broke the Southern tradition by marrying a wild rodeo cowboy from Oklahoma. My father's eating habits were a source of constant puzzlement for the young Mississippi bride, as he rejected everything from grits to mustard greens. According to my mother, before migrating to the land of milk and honey she called home, her new husband had eaten nothing but beef and dust. In desperation, she began the agonizing task of learning to make his favorite dish, chili.

Her first attempts included every pungent garden vegetable plus a little meat and red pepper. Nix after nix pared the dish down to meat and seasonings, or as my mother puts it, beef and dust.

I guess the old prairie dog knows his chili because the result of all those rejections will put any other chili out to pasture. I have made this recipe with venison because it's low in fat, but feel free to use a lean ground beef. If you use beef, be sure to pour off the grease before adding the water and seasonings.

¼ cup canola oil
3 pounds ground venison
1 quart plus 2 cups water
10 garlic cloves, minced
10 tablespoons chili powder
1 teaspoon ground cumin
1 teaspoon ground marjoram
1 teaspoon cayenne pepper

1 tablespoon sugar
3 tablespoons paprika
3 tablespoons flour
6 tablespoons cornmeal
1 teaspoon granulated beef bouillon
2 teaspoons salt, or to taste

Heat the oil in a large kettle or Dutch oven over medium heat for about 5 minutes, or until it sizzles a water droplet. Add the meat, breaking it up with a wooden spoon. Stir the meat frequently and cook it for about 12 minutes. Do not allow the meat to brown or cook too fast. It should turn a uniform gray.

Pour in 1 quart of water, turn the heat up, and bring the mixture to the boil. Add the garlic, chili powder, cumin, marjoram, cayenne, sugar, and paprika. Turn the heat down to medium and simmer for 2 hours.

Whisk the flour into 1 cup of water and stir into the chili. Next, whisk the cornmeal into the remaining 1 cup of water and stir into the chili. Add the beef bouillon granules, stir well, and salt to taste.

Serves 8

VENISON BURGERS

Ground venison is a perfect substitute for ground beef for those of you who have forsworn the latter.

2 *pounds ground venison*	**1** *garlic clove, minced*
2 *tablespoons low-sodium*	**1** *teaspoon freshly ground*
soy sauce	*black pepper*
2 *tablespoons*	
Worcestershire sauce	

Put all the ingredients in a bowl and mix well. Shape into 10 patties.

Spray a medium skillet with nonstick vegetable coating and place over medium-high heat. Cook the patties for 5 minutes on each side for rare, 8 minutes for medium-rare, and 10 minutes on each side for well-done.

Serves 10

Note: If you really like the flavor of venison, leave out all the other ingredients. These may be broiled or grilled as well.

VENISON GRILLARDS

Grillards and grits are a traditional New Orleans breakfast. Veal was commonly used in the dish, not only because of its lean and tender texture but also because it used to be quite cheap. Venison works well in grillards because it has no fat to muddy the gravy, and if you take out the cost of the hunter's Jeep, it is also quite cheap. If you're not likely to have venison in the freezer, you can substitute lean beef or veal in this recipe.

3 pounds tenderized boneless venison steak or venison tenderloin

2 garlic cloves, minced

1 cup chopped onion (about 1 large onion)

1 cup chopped green bell pepper (about 2 peppers)

1 cup chopped green onions (about 6 green onions)

½ cup Dry Roux (page 24)

1 cup water

1 cup dry red wine

2 bay leaves

2 tablespoons Worcestershire sauce

½ teaspoon Tabasco Salt and freshly ground black pepper to taste

With a sharp knife, remove any transparent connective tissue from the venison. Unless cut from the tenderloin, pound the venison with a meat mallet or the butt of a heavy drinking glass. Cut it into 3-inch strips.

Spray a large lidded skillet with nonstick vegetable coating and place over high heat. Sear the pieces of venison for about 30 seconds on each side, remove from the skillet, and set aside. Add the vegetables to the skillet all at once and turn the heat to medium. Sauté the vegetables until wilted, about 15 or 20 minutes, stirring often. Sprinkle the Dry Roux over the wilted vegetables and stir to combine. Whisk in the water and the wine until smooth. Add the remaining ingredients, including the seared meat, cover, and simmer over low heat for 1 hour. Add more water if the mixture becomes too dry. Salt and pepper to taste.

Serve hot over Grits in Bouillon (page 58).

Serves 6 to 8

Note: This dish gets better if refrigerated overnight and reheated over low heat.

VENISON SHOULDER ROAST

~~~~~~~~~~~~~~~~

This recipe calls for a shoulder roast for the simple reason that I was given this cut of meat by a sweet and generous friend; however, you may apply this method of roasting to any large piece of meat you have on hand.

1 *4- to 5-pound venison shoulder roast*

2 *garlic cloves, cut into slivers*

3 *cups burgundy or other hearty red wine*

1½ *cups low-sodium soy sauce*

½ *cup chopped fresh rosemary*

1 *medium onion, sliced*

Trim the venison of any connective tissue. Make about 12 deep slits in the roast and stuff them with garlic slivers. Mix the wine, soy sauce, rosemary, and onion, and pour over the roast. Marinate overnight, turning every now and then.

Bring the roast to room temperature. Make a fire in a barbecue with a lid, using about 5 pounds of charcoal. If using a gas grill, preheat to 325 degrees. Allow the coals to burn until white, or until you can hold your palm over the coals for 5 seconds, about 40 minutes. Soak hickory or pecan chips in water for about 1 hour.

Scatter the wood chips over the hot coals or add them to gas grill according to manufacturer's directions. Insert a meat thermometer and place the roast in the middle of the grid, directly over the coals. Roast, covered, for 20 minutes per pound or until meat thermometer reaches 170 degrees for medium-rare.

Serves 12

VENISON MEDALLIONS WITH TARRAGON

~~~~~~~~~~~~~~~~~~~~~~~~~~~~~~~~

Venison tenderloin is similar in size to pork tenderloin. These cuts of meat are entirely lean and naturally tender.

½ cup dry red wine
2 tablespoons low-sodium soy sauce
2 tablespoons Worcestershire sauce
2 garlic cloves, minced
1 medium onion, sliced
¼ teaspoon ground thyme
2 venison tenderloins, about 1 pound each
1½ cups fresh bread crumbs
1 tablespoon chopped fresh tarragon

½ teaspoon salt
1 teaspoon freshly ground black pepper, or more as needed
1 teaspoon margarine
1 teaspoon canola oil
2 tablespoons light sour cream
Chopped fresh parsley, for garnish

Mix the first 6 ingredients and pour over the tenderloins. Cover and refrigerate for at least 6 hours or overnight. Turn occasionally.

Drain the meat and strain the marinade, reserving the liquid. Remove any connective tissue from the meat with a sharp knife. Slice the venison into 1-inch-thick medallions and set aside.

Mix the bread crumbs, tarragon, salt, and pepper. Place a sheet of wax paper conveniently close to the stovetop and pour the bread crumb mixture onto it. Heat the margarine and oil in a nonstick skillet over medium-high heat until the margarine begins to foam. Dredge the medallions in the bread crumb mixture and place fairly close together in the skillet. Cook for 3½ minutes on each side, until medium-rare. Remove the meat from the skillet and keep warm.

Pour ½ cup of the marinade into the hot skillet and stir to deglaze the pan. Reduce this by half, allowing the liquid to boil for about 5 minutes. Remove the skillet from the heat and whisk in the sour cream.

To serve, spoon a little of the sauce onto each plate and place the meat on top. Garnish with fresh parsley and add black pepper to taste. Serve 3 or 4 medallions per person.

Serves 6

V ENISON T ENDERLOIN

This devilishly easy recipe may be served hot or cold, dressed with a condiment or plain. For a party, slice it thin and serve it on toast points with condiments, or eat it as my family does: as soon as it comes out of the oven.

2 *venison tenderloins,*
about 1 pound each
2 *teaspoons canola oil*

3 *tablespoons freshly*
ground black pepper

Preheat the oven to 450 degrees. Remove any connective tissue from the meat with a sharp knife. Let the tenderloins come to room temperature.

Heat 1 teaspoon of canola oil in a small skillet over high heat. Sear the tenderloins on all sides, about 1 minute per side. Remove from heat and cover with the black pepper. Place in the oven and cook for 8 minutes.

Let the meat rest for 5 to 10 minutes, then slice into medallions. The meat will be quite pink in the center.

Serves 6 to 8

Note: You can marinate these tenderloins in the same marinade as shown in the recipe for Venison Medallions with Tarragon (page 132), if desired.

Pot Liquor *and* Po' Greens

CHILE', dem sho' some po' greens! Dat pot lik-kah ain't got enough grease to float a fly!" This is what Booze said when he saw the pot of mustard greens I had simmering in chicken stock.

"Yeah," I said, "but these are better for you."

"There ain't nothin' better for you than bacon grease," piped Mama Lady. "It keeps your joints from squeakin'."

"You's right as rain, Miz Lady, I ain't never hoid none a yo' peoples' jerints a-squeakin'!" said Booze.

I marched out of the kitchen, knowing that I would never convince those two that bacon grease won't cure arthritis.

Such unhealthful traditions haunt Southern cooks. Vegetables traditionally are flavored with salt pork and sugar, which render a wonderful-tasting broth known as pot liquor. *Liquor* is a term of honor and endearment, since the actual intoxicant is consumed any time of the day or night in our neck of the woods. Po' greens means poor greens. Only the very poor went without some kind of meat in their greens. If Mama Lady and Booze were alive and looking over my shoulder, they would whine and moan for the lack of salt pork. They might not miss the grease, but they would certainly be embarrassed by the status of my po' greens.

Greens are only one of many Southern garden vegetables grown with the utmost pride, then cooked beyond recognition in butter and salt pork. The recipes in this chapter are full of flavor and brimming with rich broths seasoned with onion, garlic, and herbs instead of fat.

Corn in the Skillet

Butter Beans with Dill

Oven "Fried" Okra

Eggplant Soufflé

**Snap Beans
with Rosemary**

**Field Peas with
Fresh Tomatoes**

**Clara Brown's
Black-Eyed Peas**

Corn Pudding Soufflé

Honey Stewed Tomatoes

Lady Peas with Celery

**Collard Greens
with Onions**

**Country Glazed Carrots
without Butter**

**Okra, Corn,
and Tomatoes**

**Mustard Greens
in Chicken Broth**

**Turnip-Green Pot Pie
with a Cornmeal Crust**

Stir-Fried Greens

**Yellow Crookneck Squash
with Oven-Browned Onions**

Sweet Potato Soufflé

CORN IN THE SKILLET

~~~~~~~~~~~~~~~~

I like this dish for the sticky crust that forms along the edges. When I was a child, Mama Lady knew not to leave me unattended with a plate of skillet corn, for when she returned all that would remain would be the warm center.

4 cups corn kernels (about
8 ears), cut from the
cob, with milk reserved
1 teaspoon salt

1 teaspoon freshly ground
black pepper
2 tablespoons all-purpose
flour

Preheat a nonstick skillet over medium-high heat. At the same time, preheat the broiler.

Mix all the ingredients and pour into the hot skillet, patting down with the back of a spoon to cover the bottom of the skillet evenly. Cook over medium-high heat for 6 minutes. Place under broiler for 2 minutes or until browned on top.

Run a knife around the edge of the skillet and turn out the corn round whole or cut in wedges like a pie. Serve immediately. This will be crunchy on the outside and soft on the inside.

Serves 8

BUTTER BEANS WITH DILL

~~~~~~~~~~~~~~~~

Butter beans come in all colors and sizes. Beware of the large speckled variety—I call them the pit bulls of butter beans. They are quite tough and must be simmered all day to tame the strong flavor. The mellow flavor of the small green variety blends well with dill, and they needn't be cooked too long.

2 cups fresh or frozen
small green butter beans
1 cup Defatted Chicken
Stock (page 20)

¼ teaspoon salt
1 tablespoon chopped
fresh dill, or 1 teaspoon
dried dill

Place all the ingredients in a 2-quart saucepan over medium-high heat. Bring to the boil and lower the heat to medium-low, cover, and simmer for 30 minutes until beans are tender but not mushy. Serve hot. I like these with a traditional summer all-vegetable dinner or with ham.

Serves 8

OVEN "FRIED" OKRA

~~~~~~~~~~~~~~~~~~~~~~

One of the many gifts the New World received from Africa is okra. This vegetable is used far and wide in Southern cooking. *Gumbo* is the African word for okra, and although it is used to thicken gumbo and soups, my favorite way to eat okra is fried. These are delicious as a snack, hors d'oeuvre, or side dish. They are also a great way to introduce okra to children.

This method of oven "frying" eliminates the calories and the mess of the deep-fat fryer.

1 *egg*
¼ *teaspoon Tabasco*
1 *cup fine bread crumbs*
1 *teaspoon salt, or more as needed*
1 *teaspoon freshly ground black pepper*

1 *pound young fresh okra, washed, stemmed, and cut into ½-inch pieces*

Preheat the oven to 450 degrees. Spray a baking sheet with nonstick vegetable coating. Set aside.

In a bowl, beat the egg and Tabasco together. Combine the bread crumbs with the salt and pepper in a separate bowl. Place the okra in the bowl with the egg mixture and coat it well. Remove the okra with a slotted spoon, allowing the excess egg to drip back into the bowl, then toss the wet okra in the bread crumb mixture until well coated. Spread okra out on the prepared baking sheet and bake for 10 minutes, until golden brown. Add more salt and pepper if desired. Continue until all the okra is "fried." Serve immediately.

Serves 6 to 8

EGGPLANT SOUFFLÉ

I love eggplant any way I can get it: baked, stuffed, in pot pie, in casseroles, and, of course, fried. This recipe takes advantage of the rich flavor of the eggplant without adding any unnecessary calories. It is a delicious side dish to ham or seafood.

2 *medium eggplants*
Salt
1 *tablespoon canola oil*
  (optional)
1 *cup chopped red onion*
1 *cup chopped green bell*
  pepper
1 *teaspoon chopped fresh*
  oregano, or ¼ teaspoon
  dried oregano

1 *egg yolk*
2 *teaspoons lemon juice*
3 *tablespoons grated*
  Parmesan cheese
½ *teaspoon pepper*
1 *tablespoon bread crumbs*
3 *egg whites*

Preheat the oven to 425 degrees. Spray a baking sheet with nonstick vegetable coating and set aside.

Slice the eggplants in half lengthwise, and sprinkle the inside of each half with a little salt. Allow the eggplant to sweat on paper towels for about 20 minutes.

Place the eggplant cut side down on the prepared baking sheet and bake for 40 minutes, until quite soft. Remove the eggplant from the oven and scoop out the pulp. Discard the skins and set pulp aside.

Heat the oil (if using) in a 10-inch skillet over medium heat. Add the onion and pepper and sauté for about 15 minutes, or until onion is translucent. Add the eggplant pulp and the oregano to the skillet, and sauté for 10 more minutes. Transfer the hot vegetables to a bowl and beat in, with an electric mixer, the egg yolk, lemon juice, 2 tablespoons Parmesan cheese, ¼ teaspoon salt, and the pepper. Cover the bowl and place the eggplant mixture in the refrigerator to cool.

Spray a 1-quart soufflé dish with nonstick vegetable coating and sprinkle with the bread crumbs. Whip the egg whites until stiff and carefully fold them into the cooled eggplant mixture. Turn into the prepared dish and sprinkle the top with the remaining 1 tablespoon of Parmesan cheese. Place the soufflé in the oven, and immediately turn down to 375 degrees and bake for 25 minutes, until firm but not dry. The top will get quite brown.

Serves 8

SNAP BEANS WITH ROSEMARY

We call green beans "snaps" because of the noise they make when you break off the ends and break them in half. This used to be one of my favorite childhood kitchen duties. Mama Lady would put a big crock bowl in my lap and a paper sack of snap beans on the floor in front of me, and I would proceed to sadistically pop the "heads" and "tails" off these helpless beans. This made a delightful sound and kept my twisted little head occupied for at least half an hour.

I love the flavor of fresh rosemary with snap beans. I use this recipe as the basis for any green bean salad or side dish.

1 *tablespoon chopped fresh rosemary*
Salt to taste
1 *pound fresh young snap beans, washed*

1 *tablespoon fresh lemon juice*
Freshly ground black pepper to taste

Fill a 1½-quart saucepan with cold water and bring to a boil over high heat. While it is heating, add the rosemary and just enough salt to taste (about ¼ teaspoon). Snap off both ends of the beans and break in half. The moment the water boils, drop all the beans in and boil, uncovered, for about 8 minutes or until tender but still slightly crisp.

As soon as the beans are done, drain and toss them with a few ice cubes to stop the cooking. Pat the beans dry and toss them with the lemon juice and black pepper to taste. Serve immediately.

Serves 8

FIELD PEAS WITH FRESH TOMATOES

In summer the farmers' markets are full of peas. You cannot turn around without bumping into a bushel of these long, lavender-hulled legumes. But you'd better buy them as soon as you bump into that bushel because the next time you turn around they will have disappeared as quick as snow from a Southern sidewalk. When cooked fresh from the garden, these peas have a flavor that cannot be matched. I have a Southern friend in New York City who insisted that I tote an ice chest full of field peas on the flight from Mississippi to La Guardia Airport, just so he could savor that earthy pot liquor. I didn't blame him a bit.

These peas are, of course, usually cooked with a little leftover ham or salt pork. One way of getting around those calories is to make a broth from a ham bone that has been trimmed of all its fat, then refrigerate the broth and defat it as you would chicken broth. If that is too much bother, just cook the peas in chicken broth—they really don't need that added ham flavor. The fresh tomatoes are usually served on the side with a slathering of mayonnaise; however, I chop the tomatoes and add them to the peas at the table just to be different.

1 pound fresh purple-hull field peas, shelled	**½** teaspoon salt (optional) Freshly ground black pepper to taste
4 cups Defatted Chicken Stock (page 20) or ham stock	**4** ripe medium tomatoes, peeled and chopped

Place the peas, stock, and salt if desired in a large saucepan and bring to the boil over high heat. Lower the heat and simmer, covered, for 35 minutes. To test for doneness, smash a pea with your tongue onto the roof of your mouth. If it collapses with ease, it is done. If you like a thick pot liquor, allow the peas to cook for an hour or more until they begin to burst.

Serve the peas in a bowl, topped with black pepper and chopped tomatoes, or as a side dish.

Serves 2 fanatics or 8 Yankees

CLARA BROWN'S BLACK-EYED PEAS

~~~~~~~~~~~~~~~~~~~~~~~~~~~~~~~~~~~~~

My catering partner, Clara Nell Brown, gave me the recipe for these zippy black-eyed peas. They can, of course, be eaten by themselves but are also flavorful enough to serve with rice.

1 *pound fresh or frozen black-eyed peas*

3 *cups water or Defatted Chicken Stock (page 20)*

½ *teaspoon salt*

1 *tablespoon chopped fresh basil, or 1 teaspoon dried basil*

1 *tablespoon extra-virgin olive oil*

½ *cup chopped red bell pepper*

½ *cup chopped yellow bell pepper*

¼ *cup sliced jalapeño peppers*

Place the peas, water or stock, salt, and basil in a 2-quart saucepan over high heat and bring to the boil. Lower the heat and simmer, uncovered, for 20 minutes or until the peas are tender but not mushy. Drain the peas and set aside.

Heat the oil over medium-high heat in a skillet large enough to hold the peas. Add the sweet peppers to the hot oil and sauté for 5 to 7 minutes. Carefully fold the peas and jalapeños into the peppers, trying not to break the peas. Serve immediately.

Serves 8

CORN PUDDING SOUFFLÉ

~~~~~~~~~~~~~

The word *pudding* rarely evokes thoughts of a light dish, and Southern corn pudding usually lives up to its heavy, creamy name. This version, however, combines the rich flavor of the corn and milk with the airy texture of a soufflé. The dish is just as satisfying without the extra calories. It adds an elegant touch to menus centered on traditional Southern meats like ham, pork loin, or venison.

> **8** *ears young corn, kernels cut from the cob and cobs scraped for milk (about 5 cups of pulp)*
> **1¾** *cups evaporated skim milk*
> **1** *tablespoon margarine*
> **2** *egg yolks*
>
> **½** *teaspoon salt*
> **¼** *teaspoon freshly ground black pepper*
> **½** *teaspoon sugar*
> **1** *tablespoon cornstarch*
> **1** *tablespoon water*
> **5** *egg whites*

Spray a 2-quart soufflé dish with nonstick vegetable coating and set aside.

Place the corn, skim milk, and margarine in a heavy saucepan and bring to a steaming simmer over low heat. Cook for 25 minutes, stirring often, then remove from the heat. The mixture will be thickened.

In a separate bowl, beat the egg yolks until lemon colored. Mix a little of the hot corn mixture into the yolks to warm them, then stir into the hot corn mixture. Add the salt, pepper, and sugar. Mix the cornstarch with the water and stir this into the corn mixture. Place in the refrigerator to cool completely, about 20 minutes.

Preheat the oven to 400 degrees.

When the mixture has cooled, whip the egg whites until stiff and fold them into the corn mixture. Pour the soufflé into the prepared dish and place in the preheated oven. Immediately reduce the heat to 350 degrees and bake for 30 minutes, or until a knife, inserted, comes out clean. Serve immediately.

Serves 8

HONEY STEWED TOMATOES

Ninety-eight degrees in the shade is no exaggeration for Southern summers. Summertime is truly "dog days" down here because we wear the humidity like a coat of fur and walk around with our tongues hanging out. Dogs lie as flat and still as possible from the middle of July through August. On these long sultry days, even hungry field hands prefer a light meal, so traditionally, Southern cooks omit meats and serve vegetable buffets instead.

Stewed tomatoes are one of those vegetables that could be cooked in 20 minutes but have always been simmered for hours. If the tomatoes are sweet, ripe, homegrown beauties, let them stew a while before adding the honey; you may not need as much. (I tried the best available tomatoes at the supermarket and they needed every drop.)

Stewed tomatoes may be served as a condiment with an entrée or—as I like them—all by themselves with a big piece of cornbread.

8 *ripe large tomatoes*	*Salt and freshly ground*
¼ *cup honey, or to taste*	*black pepper to taste*

Fill a 2-quart saucepan with water and bring to a boil over high heat. Blanch the tomatoes in the boiling water for about 30 seconds, drain, and peel them. Remove the seeds and chop the pulp. You should have about 4 cups.

Place the tomato pulp and the honey in a 2-quart saucepan over medium heat and bring just to a simmer. Cook the tomatoes slowly for about 20 minutes, stirring often to prevent scorching. Salt and pepper the tomatoes to taste; I like lots of black pepper.

Serves 8

LADY PEAS WITH CELERY

It is but fair to say that, after eating my weight in various leguminous seeds, the Lady pea is the true pearl of all Southern peas. Although it resembles its common sister, the Cream pea, it is far more delicate in size, color, and flavor. Tiny Lady peas come but once a year, and although they freeze well, I've never known anyone to have any leftovers.

This recipe combines celery with the peas instead of the strong flavor of the more usual salt pork.

1 *pound Lady peas, shelled*	1 *tablespoon margarine*
2 *cups Defatted Chicken Stock (page 20)*	*Salt and freshly ground black pepper to taste*
1 *cup finely chopped celery*	

Place the peas, stock, celery, and margarine in a 2-quart saucepan over medium-high heat. Bring to a gentle simmer and cook, uncovered, for 25 minutes or until the peas are tender but not mushy. Salt and pepper the peas to taste. Serve immediately.

Serves 8

COLLARD GREENS WITH ONIONS

I have been told by a number of roadside fruit and vegetable vendors that the best time to buy and eat greens is right after the first frost. Judging from the summer collards that I find in the supermarket, which can be used for wallpaper, the early fall greens are delicate in comparison. Collards can be slightly bitter even at their peak, so this recipe calls for just a touch of brown sugar. (Cooked greens freeze well and are a wonderful source of iron and calcium. Freeze them with their broth in airtight freezer bags. They will keep for several months.)

4 tablespoons safflower oil
2 cups chopped onions
2 tablespoons light brown
   sugar
4 pounds small young
   collard greens (see Note,
   page 149)

2 cups Defatted Chicken
   Stock (page 20)

In a large kettle, heat the oil over medium heat, add the onions, and sauté for about 20 minutes. Add the brown sugar and stir until dissolved. Fold in the wet collard greens and add the stock. Cover and simmer about 1 hour or until tender. All greens cook down to about one-fourth of the original bulk, so don't be surprised. Serve hot.

Serves 8 to 10

COUNTRY GLAZED CARROTS WITHOUT BUTTER

If you can find young, sweet spring carrots, you might want to cut the sugar in half. These go well with pork.

2 pounds carrots, peeled
   and sliced into rings
½ cup water
2 tablespoons cornstarch
4 tablespoons light brown
   sugar

4 tablespoons lemon juice
   Salt and freshly ground
   black pepper to taste

In a large saucepan, bring 2 quarts of water to the boil and add the carrots. Blanch over high heat for about 5 minutes, then drain and return the carrots to the saucepan. Mix the water, cornstarch, brown sugar, and lemon juice in a small bowl with a fork or a wire whisk and pour over the carrots. Cook the carrots with the sauce over medium heat, stirring constantly until thickened, about 10 minutes. Season with salt and pepper. Serve immediately.

Serves 8

OKRA, CORN, AND TOMATOES

In the summer, there is no escape from this prevalent combination of garden vegetables. It lurks on every luncheon buffet and cafeteria in the South, and I for one am always glad for the large serving spoons available. I like this dish served with poultry, but Down South it is appreciated as a side dish to almost anything.

This recipe uses the natural juices of the vegetables instead of bacon grease or butter for cooking.

6 ripe medium tomatoes
1 medium onion, chopped
2 cups okra, sliced in ½-inch pieces (about 24 small pods)
1 cup corn kernels, scraped from the cob and with milk reserved (about 4 young ears)

½ teaspoon sugar (if desired)
Salt and freshly ground black pepper to taste

Fill a 2-quart saucepan with water and bring to the boil over high heat. Blanch the tomatoes in the boiling water for about 30 seconds, drain, and remove the skins. Seed and chop the tomatoes. You should have about 2 cups.

Place the tomatoes in a large saucepan over medium heat and bring to a simmer. Add the onion and cook for about 10 minutes, until transparent. Add the okra, corn, sugar if desired, and salt and pepper. Cover and simmer the vegetables for about 20 minutes or until the corn is tender, stirring often. Serve immediately.

Serves 8

Note: If the vegetables dry out before becoming tender, add a little water or chicken stock to prevent any scorching.

MUSTARD GREENS IN CHICKEN BROTH

~~~~~~~~~~~~~~~~~~~~~~~~~~~~~~~~~~~~~

Downtown Natchez is a sleepy garden of big, ornate mansions and tiny jewels of Victorian gingerbread. Each house, no matter how modest, is wrapped in a cloak of azalea bushes, crepe myrtle trees, camellias, oleanders, gardenias, untamed vines, and other flowers. Huge oaks and magnolias shade the gardens and rooftops with their protective, moss-draped limbs and shiny leaves. Inside these houses one is confronted with the Southerner's nonchalant yet tenacious family pride: an heirloom silver tea service sits on top of the refrigerator, a hand-painted china saucer from Paris is used as an ashtray, a Civil War sword leans against the TV set.

Although these mementos of antebellum wealth set these city dwellers apart from their sharecropping cousins, the food they enjoy is exactly the same. Whether you are handed a crock bowl in the kitchen or sit down to a sterling silver serving plate with a damask napkin in your lap, you can bet on being served mustard greens if they're in season.

> 4 tablespoons safflower or
>   canola oil
> ½ teaspoon minced garlic
> 8 bunches mustard greens
>   (see Note)
>
> 2 cups Defatted Chicken
>   Stock (page 20)
> ½ teaspoon sugar
>   Salt and freshly ground
>   pepper to taste

In a large kettle, heat the oil over medium heat and sauté the garlic for about 5 minutes; be careful not to let the garlic brown. Fold the wet greens into the hot oil, then add the stock and sugar. Cover, turn the heat to medium-low, and simmer the greens for about 45 minutes or until tender. Salt and pepper, to taste. Serve immediately.

Serves 8

Note: Look for small greens in the grocery store—the large ones are usually very tough. To kill any lurking bugs and wash off soil, fill the sink with cool water and immerse the greens. Sprinkle with about 1 tablespoon of salt and swish the greens in the saltwater for about 1 minute. Rinse, stem, and chop the greens but do not dry them.

TURNIP-GREEN POT PIE WITH A CORNMEAL CRUST

~~~~~~~~~~~~~~~~

You can't get much more Southern than this!

Cornmeal Crust

1 cup all-purpose flour
½ cup yellow cornmeal
¼ teaspoon salt

1 cup (2 sticks) plus
1 tablespoon frozen
margarine, cut into
18 pieces
5 tablespoons ice water

Turnip Green Filling

1½ cups Defatted Chicken
Stock (page 20)
1 cup chopped onion

2 garlic cloves, chopped
4 pounds turnip greens
(see Note, page 149)

To make the crust, combine the flour, cornmeal, and salt in a large bowl or in the bowl of a food processor. Cut in the margarine with 2 knives or a pastry blender, or process with the metal processor blade until the dough resembles coarse meal. Add the ice water and stir the dough with a fork, or process until the dough holds together in a ball. If the dough seems too sticky, divide 1 tablespoon of flour between your hands and work it into the dough by tossing it lightly back and forth. Wrap the dough in plastic wrap and chill for 30 minutes.

To make the filling, bring the stock to a boil in a large pot with a lid and add the onion and garlic. Cook over medium-high heat for 10 minutes, or until the onion is transparent. Fold in the turnip greens, cover the pot, lower the heat, and simmer for 1 hour or longer (depending on their age) until the greens are tender.

Preheat the oven to 425 degrees.

Roll out the chilled dough into a 10-inch circle. Spoon the turnip greens and any juice into a 10-inch baking dish 2-inches deep. Cover the greens with the crust and bake for 20 minutes or until the crust is golden brown. Serve immediately.

Serves 8

STIR-FRIED GREENS

It is with sincere trepidation that I submit this recipe, for fear that Booze and Mama Lady will hurl lightning bolts down from the clouds. From their perch, it must seem that this child has finally gone too far, that I've stepped way over that Mason-Dixon line all the way to China. Facing this celestial ridicule with irreverence, I must say that stir-fried greens are not only the tastiest way to enjoy greens but the easiest and healthiest. (Unless you are braver than I and choose to eat them raw; in that case, turn the page!)

4 *garlic cloves*
4 *pounds turnip greens*
  (see Note, page 149)
1 *tablespoon canola oil*

2 *tablespoons low-sodium*
  soy sauce
  Vinegar (hot pepper or
  fruity) if desired

Preheat the oven to 425 degrees.

Place the garlic in a small baking dish or on a small piece of foil and bake for 20 minutes or until lightly browned on the outside and soft on the inside. Fill a 4-quart kettle with cold water and bring to a rolling boil over high heat. Drop the turnip greens into the boiling water all at once and blanch them for about 5 minutes, until bright green. Drain the greens and rinse under cold water, then drain them again.

Heat the oil in a large skillet or wok over medium-high heat until a drop of water sizzles the moment it hits the oil. Add the greens and garlic pulp by squeezing each clove until the pulp drops from its skin into the skillet. Discard the garlic skins. Add the soy sauce, then stir and toss this mixture for 10 minutes, until the greens are tender. Sprinkle vinegar over the greens.

Serves 8

YELLOW CROOKNECK SQUASH WITH OVEN-BROWNED ONIONS

〜〜〜〜〜〜〜〜〜〜〜〜〜

You can always tell a good crookneck squash from its color—it should be milky yellow with no sheen. The older they get, the shinier and darker the skin becomes. These squash are usually simmered for quite a long time with loads of butter, onions, sugar, salt, and pepper. My recipe uses the rich taste of Oven-Browned Onions instead of sugar and butter, and I steam the squash to preserve the nutrients.

8 *medium yellow crookneck squash*
2 *cups Oven-Browned Onions (recipe follows)*

1 *teaspoon salt*
2 *teaspoons freshly ground black pepper*

Rinse and slice the squash thinly. Place in a steamer and steam for about 20 minutes or until the squash is just tender. Toss the squash with the onions, salt, and pepper and serve immediately.

Serves 8

OVEN-BROWNED ONIONS

These onions brown and caramelize without any butter or oil, and can be used in anything that calls for sautéed onions. I like to keep them on hand in my freezer to throw into soups and sauces.

2 *pounds onions*

Preheat the oven to 200 degrees.

Spray a roasting pan with nonstick vegetable coating. Peel and chop (or slice, as you prefer) the onions. Spread them out in the prepared pan and roast for about 6 hours, stirring occasionally until the onions are an even caramel brown. Be careful not to leave them in too long, since they will begin to taste burned. Let cool, then freeze in ½-cup portions in airtight freezer bags, if desired.

Makes about 6 cups

SWEET POTATO SOUFFLÉ

~~~~~~~~

Southerners are extravagant people, and nowhere is this more evident than in our baroque treatment of sweet potatoes. We add butter, cream, molasses, brown sugar, nutmeg, cinnamon, eggs, and, God forbid, marshmallows. All of which, when you come right down to it, are unnecessary, especially the marshmallows, since the sweet potato is naturally rich and very sweet. In accordance with sweet potato ritual, I have left this recipe fairly fancy, but in accordance with good sense I left out the marshmallows.

5 *medium sweet potatoes*
½ *cup Oven-Browned Onions (page 152)*
2 *tablespoons (¼ stick) margarine*

½ *teaspoon salt*
½ *teaspoon freshly ground black pepper*
6 *egg whites*

Preheat the oven to 400 degrees.

Rinse the sweet potatoes under cold water and pierce each several times with a fork. Place the sweet potatoes on a baking sheet and bake for about 1 hour or until quite soft. Allow to cool for 10 minutes or so. Lower oven temperature to 375 degrees.

Spray a 2-quart soufflé dish with nonstick vegetable coating and set aside. Scoop out the sweet potato pulp and discard skins; you should have about 3 cups. With an electric mixer, beat the potato pulp and, with the mixer still running, blend in the onions, margarine, salt, and pepper. Place this mixture in the refrigerator to cool for about 20 minutes.

Beat the egg whites until stiff but not dry. When the potato mixture is cool to the touch, carefully fold in the beaten egg whites. Turn the soufflé into the prepared dish. Bake for 40 minutes or until nicely puffed and a knife, inserted in the center, comes out clean. Serve immediately.

Serves 8

A Loaf of Bread, a Jar of Fig Preserves, and . . .

S

OUTHERN autumn wind is a mild and welcome change from the standstill heat of summer. A crisp energy in the air wakes us from the sultry months past and prepares us for the winter months to come. This has long been the season for festivals, outdoor gatherings, and hearthside family dinners. Fall brings the feelings of camaraderie from school days and warmth from the loving celebration of holidays. Neighbors share their jars of preserves and jams from the fruits of summer and, it is hoped, warm biscuits and breads to go with them.

Hot bread and cool jam can't be beat, and I for one have no intention of giving up either for the sake of wearing a tight miniskirt. Without summoning Mammy to cinch my corset, I think a reasonable waistline can be maintained by creating breads that contain less fat and preserves with less sugar. Of course, we'll have to bid farewell to that divine habit of spreading our breads with thick cream or soft butter, but take heart —these recipes really *are* satisfying even without all those extra calories.

Blueberry Bread

Buttermilk Corn Bread

Braided Ham Bread

Hushpuppy Muffins

Buttermilk Biscuits

**Cornsticks with
Light Cracklins**

**Buttermilk Cornmeal
Hotcakes**

**Honey-Pecan
Corn Muffins**

Sour Cream Biscuits

Yeast Cornmeal Rolls

Savory Popovers

**Whole-Kernel
Corn Bread**

**Buttermilk
Icebox Rolls**

**Sweet Potato
Pecan Bread**

BLUEBERRY BREAD

~~~~~~~~~~~~~~~~~~~~~~~~~~

The first thing to remember when making yeast breads is not to be afraid of putting your hands in the dough, and the second thing is not to be in any kind of hurry.

This bread has a moist fruit filling containing no sugar, eliminating the need for jam or butter.

2 *cups water*
4 *tablespoons (½ stick) margarine*
4 *cups all-purpose flour*
1 *package active dry yeast*
2 *teaspoons salt*

½ *cup light brown sugar*
½ *cup honey*
1 *egg*
   Grated zest of 1 lemon (optional)
2 *cups whole wheat flour*

Filling

2 *cups fresh blueberries*
3 *tablespoons white grape juice concentrate, thawed*

1½ *teaspoons ground cinnamon*
3 *tablespoons all-purpose flour*

Spray two 1½-quart loaf pans with nonstick vegetable coating.

Combine the water and margarine in a saucepan and heat just until the margarine melts, or to a temperature of 110 degrees.

Sift together 2 cups of the all-purpose flour, yeast, salt, and brown sugar in a large mixing bowl. Add the water and margarine mixture, honey, egg, and lemon zest. Blend briskly and thoroughly and work in the remaining all-purpose flour and the whole wheat flour. (I use a wooden fork and plenty of elbow grease for this job, but you can also use an electric mixer with a dough hook.)

Turn the soft dough out onto a lightly floured board and knead until the dough is smooth and elastic, about 10 minutes, adding more flour as needed. Shape into a ball. Spray a clean mixing bowl with nonstick vegetable coating. Add the dough and turn it to coat all sides. Cover the bowl with plastic wrap and let it stand in a warm, draft-free place until doubled in bulk, about 2 hours.

Turn out the dough and knead it lightly. Cover it and let it rest for 5 minutes.

To make the filling, toss all the ingredients together in a bowl until the blueberries are well coated.

Divide the dough in half and roll each half into a rectangle on a floured surface. Spread the filling over the rolled-out rectangles, leaving a 2-inch border. Roll each rectangle jelly-roll fashion and tuck under the ends. Place the dough seam side down in the prepared pans, and cover lightly with clean cloths. Return the loaves to a warm place and let stand until doubled in bulk, about 1 hour.

Preheat the oven to 375 degrees. Bake the loaves for 45 minutes. Cool in the pan for 10 minutes, then turn out onto a rack and cool completely before slicing.

Makes 2 9-inch loaves

BUTTERMILK CORN BREAD

This recipe comes from my mother's mother's side of the family. Needless to say, it is quite different from Mama Lady's corn-sticks recipe (page 163), which comes from my mother's father's mother's side of the family.

2 tablespoons canola oil	**2½** teaspoons sugar
1 cup yellow cornmeal	**1** egg
¾ cup self-rising flour	**1** cup buttermilk
1 teaspoon salt	
1½ teaspoons baking powder	

Preheat the oven to 425 degrees. Coat the bottom and sides of an iron skillet with 1 tablespoon of oil. Place the skillet in the oven while you mix the batter.

Mix the dry ingredients. Stir in the egg, milk, and remaining oil until completely moistened. Pour into the hot skillet and bake for 25 minutes or until golden brown.

Serves 8

Note: For a change, try adding ground nuts or a spice like cumin to your next batch.

BRAIDED HAM BREAD

I like to serve this bread for breakfast, especially if we have houseguests. It's great to just leave out and let your guests grab a piece as they rise. And for those of you who celebrate Mardi Gras with a king cake, try this instead of the very sweet traditional cake—but remember to add the plastic baby doll!

1 cup low-fat milk
3 tablespoons honey
3 tablespoons margarine
1 teaspoon salt
1½ packages active dry yeast

3½ cups all-purpose flour
2 eggs
1 tablespoon chopped fresh basil leaves

Filling

1 cup chopped onion
1 cup chopped turkey ham

2 cups low-fat cheese, such as part-skim mozzarella or reduced-fat Cheddar

Combine the milk, honey, margarine, and salt in a saucepan. Heat until the margarine melts. Let cool to lukewarm and stir in the yeast.

Place the flour in the container of a food processor. Mix in the eggs and basil. With the motor running, add the yeast mixture through the feed tube. Process the dough until a ball forms and the dough pulls away from the sides of the container. Add more flour if the dough sticks to the sides of the bowl. Turn the dough out onto a lightly floured board and knead briefly, about 1 minute. Shape the dough into a ball and put it in a bowl that has been sprayed with nonstick vegetable coating. Turn dough to coat all sides, then cover with a damp towel and let stand in a warm draft-free place until doubled in bulk, about 1 hour.

To make the filling, place the onion and turkey ham in a nonstick skillet over medium heat and sauté for about 15 minutes or until the onion is translucent. Remove from the heat and toss with the cheese.

Punch down the dough. Knead briefly and shape into a small rectangle with your fingertips. Roll the dough into a 12-×-8 inch rectangle; the dough should be quite thin. Cut the rectangle into 3 strips and divide the filling evenly over each strip, leaving about a 2-inch border. Close each strip by folding the ends over the filling and pinching together the seams. Place the strips seam side down on a baking sheet sprayed with nonstick vegetable coating and braid the strips, tucking the ends under. Cover with a damp towel and allow the braid to rise in a warm place for another hour.

Preheat the oven to 350 degrees and bake the bread for about 35 minutes. If the bread looks too brown, cover it with aluminum foil and continue to bake.

Makes 1 large loaf

HUSHPUPPY MUFFINS

~~~~~~~~~~~

Hushpuppies are little fried balls of cornmeal batter supposedly once tossed at an irritating beggar of a dog during a campfire fish fry. Over the years they have sometimes been more of a hit than the fish they were meant to accompany. This recipe eliminates the frying and produces a crisp, nongreasy muffin.

1 cup yellow cornmeal	3 tablespoons minced
Scant ¼ teaspoon dried	green onions
ground thyme	1 cup boiling water
½ teaspoon sugar	1 egg, beaten
¼ teaspoon cayenne	1 tablespoon margarine,
pepper	melted
1 teaspoon salt	Dash of Tabasco

Preheat the oven to 500 degrees. Spray a small-cup muffin tin with nonstick vegetable coating.

Mix the dry ingredients, including onions, with a fork. Make a well in the center and pour in the boiling water. Stir briskly. Stir in the beaten egg, margarine, and Tabasco. Spoon about 2 tablespoons of batter into each muffin cup. Bake for 15 to 20 minutes or until golden brown on top.

Makes 1 dozen small muffins

Note: For an even spicier flavor, serve with margarine that has been whipped with a teaspoon or more of Tabasco.

BUTTERMILK BISCUITS

The only time I ever saw my great-grandmother, Mama Lady, remove her wedding band was when she was going to "throw together some biscuits." Actually, "throw" is much too violent a term for the light toss from palm to palm she used to shape her fluffy, angelic breads. I used to think of her biscuits as mere vessels for preserves until I tried someone else's biscuits. I realized how easy it is to make a tough mess of a simple dough. Remember that the less you handle the dough, the better the biscuits.

This recipe allows you to use margarine or oil instead of shortening or butter. Margarine produces an airy biscuit because the solid pieces leave air holes as they melt. Oil produces a light, cakey biscuit because the oil is distributed evenly throughout the dough.

2½ *cups all-purpose flour*
1 *teaspoon salt (or ½ teaspoon if using margarine)*
4 *teaspoons baking powder*

3 *tablespoons canola oil or margarine*
⅞ *cup buttermilk*

In a large bowl, mix 1½ cups of the flour, salt, and baking powder with a fork. Add the oil and stir quickly until the mixture resembles coarse meal. (If you use margarine, cut the margarine into the dry ingredients with 2 knives or a pastry blender.) Add the buttermilk all at once and stir with a fork just until the batter is moistened. The batter will look lumpy and feel sticky.

Preheat the oven to 500 degrees. Spray a baking sheet with nonstick vegetable coating.

Place the remaining cup of flour in another large bowl. Dust your hands well with flour, then pinch off a piece of dough the size of a ping-pong ball. Drop it into the flour to coat it. Toss it back and forth, from one hand to the other once, then place it gently on the prepared baking sheet. Pat the top down gently to give it a smooth shape. Dust off any excess flour with a dry paper towel. Place the biscuits close together and bake for 10 minutes. Serve hot.

Makes 12 to 18 biscuits

CORNSTICKS WITH LIGHT CRACKLINS

~~~~~~~~~~~~~~~~~~~~~~~~~~~~~~~~

Cornstick pans are as common in Southern kitchens as fly swat-ters. They are oblong cast-iron pans with separate slots that mold the batter into small ears of corn. Mama Lady used these pans when, as she would say, she had time to think about it. In the usual kitchen flurry, she would simply grab her trusty black iron skillet.

Another common fixture in Southern kitchens is an old coffee can that sits on the shelf over the stove and stores leftover bacon grease. Booze used bacon grease to flavor anything from corn bread to fresh greens. This recipe captures the flavor of the bacon and leaves the grease behind.

2½ *tablespoons canola oil*	**1** *teaspoon salt*
8 *strips lean bacon*	**1** *egg*
2 *cups yellow cornmeal*	**1½** *cups buttermilk*
4 *teaspoons baking powder*	

Preheat the oven to 450 degrees. Pour ½ teaspoon of oil into each slot of 2 cast-iron cornstick pans (see Note). Place the pans in the oven until ready to fill.

To make light cracklins, blanch the bacon in boiling water for 5 minutes. Remove with a slotted spoon and pat dry. Fry in a skillet over medium heat until quite crisp; this renders most of the fat and salt. Drain well on paper towels. Crumble when cooled. You should have about ½ cup.

Mix the dry ingredients and cracklins lightly with a fork. Beat the egg with the buttermilk separately, then stir into the dry ingredients. Mix the batter with a fork just until all of the dry ingredients are moistened. Divide the batter among the cornstick molds and bake for 20 minutes.

Makes 16 cornsticks

Note: If you don't have cornstick pans, you can use small muffin tins. However, you need only preheat cast-iron pans. This batter can also be cooked in an 8-inch cast-iron skillet to make a large corn bread.

BUTTERMILK CORNMEAL HOTCAKES

The cornmeal adds a slightly sweet flavor to these light and fluffy hotcakes. Top them with honey-sweetened yogurt and your favorite fruit.

¾ cup yellow cornmeal
1 cup all-purpose flour
1 teaspoon baking powder
3 tablespoons sugar

½ teaspoon salt
2 cups buttermilk
2 tablespoons canola oil
4 egg whites

Sift together the dry ingredients. Set aside. Mix the buttermilk and canola oil and stir into the cornmeal mixture until well blended. Beat egg whites until soft peaks form and fold into the batter.

Heat a nonstick skillet over medium heat and spoon the batter, ¼ cup at a time, into the hot skillet. Cook for about 3½ minutes on the first side or until the surface is covered with holes. Turn the cakes with a spatula and cook for about 2 minutes until brown. Serve immediately.

Makes 12 hotcakes

HONEY-PECAN CORN MUFFINS

I love the taste of honey with cornmeal. This recipe makes a slightly sweet muffin that is great served with lean pork or chicken dishes. Try using these for making bread crumbs for stuffing.

1½ cups yellow cornmeal
1 cup all-purpose flour
4 teaspoons baking powder
1 teaspoon salt
½ cup honey

¼ cup canola oil
1 egg
1 cup low-fat milk
1 cup finely chopped pecans

Preheat the oven to 400 degrees. Spray a muffin tin with nonstick vegetable coating and set aside.

Mix the dry ingredients except the pecans in a large bowl. In a separate bowl, beat the honey, oil, egg, and milk. Make a well in the center of the dry ingredients and stir in the milk mixture. Stir in the chopped pecans. Spoon ¼ cup batter into each muffin cup and bake for 15 to 20 minutes or until puffed and golden.

Makes 12 muffins

Note: Honey-roasted nuts work well in these muffins. If you use them, reduce the amount of salt by half.

SOUR CREAM BISCUITS

These are pretty biscuits that contain no butter or oil. Be careful not to knead the dough too long, or the biscuits will be tough. I like to eat them with low-sugar jam.

3 *cups all-purpose flour*	**¾** *cup low-fat plain yogurt*
3 *teaspoons baking powder*	**4** *tablespoons (½ stick) margarine, melted*
1 *teaspoon salt*	*(optional)*
1 *cup light sour cream*	

Preheat the oven to 450 degrees. Spray a baking sheet with nonstick vegetable coating.

Sift together the dry ingredients in a large bowl. Stir in the sour cream and yogurt with a fork until all of the dough is moistened. Turn out onto a well-floured board and knead just until the dough binds, about 1 minute. Roll out to ¼ inch thick and cut with a small juice glass or 2-inch biscuit cutter. Place the biscuits fairly close together on the prepared pan. Brush the tops with melted margarine, if desired, and bake for about 8 minutes. (If you've made big biscuits, bake them for about 12 minutes or until nicely browned on top.) These biscuits are crunchy on the outside and cakey on the inside. They are best served right out of the oven.

Makes 12 to 14 biscuits

YEAST CORNMEAL ROLLS

~~~~~~~~~~~~~~~~~~~~~~~~~~~~

These are great with soup, stews, or chili.

2 *packages active dry yeast*	**½** *cup canola oil*
2 *teaspoons salt*	**2** *cups yellow cornmeal*
¼ *cup honey*	**5** *cups all-purpose flour*
2 *cups lukewarm water (110 degrees)*	

Dissolve the yeast, salt, and honey in the warm water in a large bowl. Stir in the oil. Add the cornmeal and stir well. Stir in the flour 1 cup at a time to make a soft dough.

Turn out dough onto a floured board and knead until smooth and elastic, about 10 minutes. Spray a bowl with nonstick vegetable coating and place dough in bowl, turning to coat well. Cover with a kitchen towel and let rise for 1 hour or until doubled in bulk.

Punch down the dough and knead briefly, about 1 minute. Roll out and cut into 2-inch squares. Fold the squares into little pocketbooks or envelopes and place about 1 inch apart on a baking sheet that has been sprayed with nonstick vegetable coating. Cover with a kitchen towel and put in a warm place to rise again for about 30 minutes or until doubled in bulk.

Preheat the oven to 375 degrees and bake the rolls for 15 minutes or until nicely browned on top. Serve hot.

Makes 4 dozen

SAVORY POPOVERS

~~~~~~~~~~~~~~~~~~~~~~~~~~~~

Southern popovers are usually made with at least six eggs and embellished with heavy cream and melted butter. This recipe turns out a rich, tasty popover with only a smidgen of the calories. For parties, I like to make these in small-cup muffin tins and top them with ham salad or soft herbed cheese.

2 *eggs*
¾ *cup low-fat milk*
¼ *cup water*
1 *cup all-purpose flour*

½ *teaspoon salt*
½ *teaspoon ground thyme*
  or dried dill (or your
  favorite herb)

Preheat the oven to 450 degrees. Spray 6 custard cups or a muffin tin with nonstick vegetable coating.

Place the ingredients in a blender or a food processor and blend until smooth. Fill each cup three-fourths full with batter. Bake for 15 minutes. Lower the heat to 350 degrees and bake for 20 minutes or until the popovers are crisp on the outside. Don't peek during baking. Remove from the oven and prick with a fork to allow the steam to escape. These are best served hot.

Makes 6 large popovers

WHOLE-KERNEL CORN BREAD

The whole kernels of juicy corn add more corn flavor and moisture to this recipe for fluffy corn bread.

¼ *cup canola oil*
1 *cup yellow cornmeal*
1 *cup all-purpose flour*
1 *teaspoon salt*
4 *teaspoons baking*
  powder

1 *cup buttermilk*
4 *teaspoons honey*
1 *egg*
1 *cup fresh corn kernels,*
  scraped from the cob,
  with milk reserved

Preheat the oven to 400 degrees. Pour the oil into a well-seasoned 8-inch cast-iron skillet and turn to coat the bottom and sides. Pour excess oil into a small cup and set aside. Place the oiled skillet in the oven to heat.

Combine the dry ingredients in a large bowl. Add the reserved oil, buttermilk, honey, and egg and stir well. Stir in the corn with its milk. Spoon into the hot skillet and bake for 20 to 25 minutes until corn bread is golden brown.

Serves 8

BUTTERMILK ICEBOX ROLLS

This dough keeps for about five days in the refrigerator and can be shaped into any kind of roll you like. You can reduce the amount of salt, if necessary for your diet.

2 *packages active dry yeast*
½ *cup lukewarm water (110 degrees)*
2 *cups buttermilk*
½ *cup canola oil*
½ *cup honey*
1 *tablespoon salt*
6 *to 8 cups all-purpose flour*

Combine the yeast with the warm water and let stand until it dissolves. Mix the buttermilk, oil, honey, and salt in a large bowl. Add the dissolved yeast and mix well. Stir in enough flour (about 6 cups) to make a soft dough.

Turn out onto a well-floured board and knead for about 10 minutes or until dough springs back from a light finger poke. Spray a large bowl with nonstick vegetable coating. Place the ball of dough in the bowl and turn it to coat all over. Cover with a kitchen towel and place in a warm draft-free place to rise for 1 hour.

Punch the dough down. Cover with plastic wrap and refrigerate until ready to use, or use immediately by pinching off pieces of dough and shaping the rolls however you like. Place rolls 2 inches apart on a baking sheet that has been sprayed with nonstick vegetable coating, and let rise again until doubled, about 30 minutes.

Preheat the oven to 400 degrees. Bake the rolls for 15 minutes or until lightly browned on top.

Makes several dozen rolls, depending on size

SWEET POTATO PECAN BREAD

This quick bread is great to keep around during the holidays for unexpected guests. It's not too sweet so it can be served for breakfast or with an entrée. Slice it fairly thin and heat in microwave on high for about 10 seconds a slice, for a right-out-of-the-oven taste. I like to serve this bread hot, topped with cool, ripe, sliced peaches.

2 cups peeled sweet potatoes (about 3 medium potatoes)

1 whole egg plus 2 egg whites

1 cup light brown sugar or honey

¾ cup canola oil

3 cups all-purpose flour

1 teaspoon salt

¼ teaspoon baking powder

1 teaspoon baking soda

1½ teaspoons ground cinnamon

¼ teaspoon grated nutmeg

½ cup chopped pecans

1 cup mashed ripe banana pulp (about 2 bananas)

½ cup raisins

Preheat the oven to 350 degrees. Spray a 1½-quart loaf pan with nonstick vegetable coating.

Grate the sweet potatoes and set aside. Beat the egg and whites with the brown sugar or honey until lighter in color and thickened. Beat in the oil.

Sift together the flour, salt, baking powder, soda, cinnamon, and nutmeg. Fold this into the egg mixture, then stir in the grated sweet potatoes, pecans, banana, and raisins. Spoon the mixture into the prepared pan and bake for 1 hour, or until the bread pulls away from the sides of the pan.

Makes 1 9-inch loaf

Sweet **Dreams**

SOUTHERN desserts are big, fat, and lovable. Unlike persnickety French desserts, with their spun sugar and puff pastry, there's nothing intimidating about cooking or eating rice pudding or sweet potato pie. Most of these luscious recipes are based on ingredients like eggs, butter, and fresh produce, which were abundant on plantations.

Baking desserts is not something one does only on a special occasion but an everyday occurrence, like throwing together biscuits or a pan of corn bread. My mother made a fresh pound cake every day that was pulled hot out of the oven just as my brother and I arrived home, ravenous, from school.

Perhaps it's part of the agrarian culture that seems to stick to us like sugarcane molasses. The slow pace and extravagant taste of antebellum days have left us with a strong grip on savoring sweet moments. Taking a bite of sweet, creamy fig ice cream, I am reminded of renowned Natchez citizen General John A. Quitman's timeless statement: "It is an indolent yet charming life and one quits thinking and takes to dreaming."

In this chapter I have taken the saturated fat out of traditional desserts and reduced the sugar content considerably. I have also invented a few new desserts. Like a sweet dream, these desserts will satisfy your sweet tooth and disappear with the last bite, leaving no visible evidence except a contented smile.

Light Bananas Foster

Wild Plum Soufflé

Café-au-Lait Chiffon Pie

Watermelon Ice

Spiced Pecan Drop Cookies

Peach Rice Pudding

Gingerbread

Blackberry Mousse

Buttermilk Sherbet

Chocolate Angel Food Cake

Strawberry Sherbet

Mama Lady's One-Layer Spice Cake

Pecan-Honey Candy

Sweet Potato Cake with Ricotta Filling

Sweet Potato Pie

Banana Cream Pie

LIGHT BANANAS FOSTER

Bananas Foster was born and gained its fame in old New Orleans restaurants. Always prepared at tableside, this dish is a source of pride for veteran waiters all over the French Quarter. When you prepare it at home, do it justice and wear a tux.

1 tablespoon margarine
1 tablespoon frozen apple juice concentrate, thawed
1 tablespoon light brown sugar
Pinch of ground cinnamon

1 ripe banana, quartered lengthwise
1 ounce (2 tablespoons) banana liqueur
1 ounce (2 tablespoons) rum

In a chafing dish or small skillet over medium-high heat, melt the margarine. Add the apple juice concentrate, brown sugar, and cinnamon and stir about 2 minutes until the sugar melts.

Add the banana slices and sauté 1 minute, turning the pieces carefully to coat them with the sauce. Add the liqueur and rum and ignite. Stir the mixture in a flamboyant manner to encourage the flames. When the flames die down, spoon the fruit and sauce over vanilla ice milk or vanilla frozen yogurt.

Serves 2

Note: I do not recommend increasing this recipe to feed more than 2 at a time, since the flames might grow with the amount of sauce and cause your drapes to curl toward the ceiling, leaving ashes on the carpet. If you are feeding more than 2 people, make the dish as many times as necessary.

WILD PLUM SOUFFLÉ

Every time Mama Lady cooked anything sweet, my brother and I would sit on kitchen stools and stare at the batter-laden spoons like hungry dogs. One of the first things I remember tasting from a big cooking spoon was the soft pink foam that Mama Lady skimmed from a boiling kettle of wild plum jelly.

This soufflé, with its light, airy texture and pungent fruit taste, is reminiscent of that same foam I longed to capture and put up in jars, just as Mama Lady put up her clear, tart jelly. If you can't find wild plums in your neck of the woods, select any tart domestic plum.

12 *large, ripe plums*
2 *tablespoons (¼ stick)*
   margarine
½ *cup sugar*

1 *ounce (2 tablespoons)*
   dry sherry
8 *egg whites*

Preheat the oven to 400 degrees. Spray a 2-quart soufflé dish with nonstick vegetable coating and set aside.

Bring 2 quarts of water to the boil and blanch the plums for about 45 seconds or until the skins begin to wrinkle. Drain the plums in a colander and let them cool. When they are cool enough to handle, peel them, remove the pits, and slice in ⅛-inch slices. You should have about 5 cups of pulp.

Melt the margarine in a large skillet over medium-high heat and add the plum pulp and the sugar. Cook, stirring for about 10 minutes, until thickened. Add the sherry to the skillet and cook for 5 minutes more.

Remove the skillet from the heat and puree the cooked plums in a food processor, blender, or food mill, or mash by hand with a potato masher. Cover the puree and place it in the refrigerator until cool, about 20 minutes.

Whip the egg whites until soft peaks form. Fold the egg whites into the cooled puree. The mixture should be a light apricot color with specks of white and some streaks of fruit. Do not overmix the batter. Turn the batter into the prepared dish and place in the oven. Immediately reduce the heat to 375 degrees and bake for 30 minutes. Serve immediately.

Serves 8

CAFÉ-AU-LAIT CHIFFON PIE

I make this pie with my favorite blend of French roast coffee, but I think it's fun to experiment with different blends in any recipe that calls for coffee.

Crust

- ¼ cup finely ground pecans
- 1 cup graham cracker crumbs
- 2 tablespoons confectioners' sugar
- ¼ teaspoon ground cinnamon
- 2 tablespoons (¼ stick) margarine, melted

Filling

- 1 envelope unflavored gelatin
- ½ cup skim milk
- 1 cup strong brewed French roast coffee
- ⅓ cup plus 5 tablespoons sugar
- 2 eggs, whites separated and yolks lightly beaten
- 1 teaspoon vanilla extract
- ¼ teaspoon ground cinnamon
- ⅓ cup water
- ⅓ cup nonfat dry milk
- 1 cup finely chopped pecans

To make the crust, mix the nuts and dry ingredients and add the margarine. Combine thoroughly, making sure that the dry ingredients are well moistened. Press firmly into the bottom and sides of a 10-inch pie plate and place in the freezer while you prepare the filling.

To make the filling, sprinkle the gelatin over ¼ cup of the milk and let stand for 1 minute. Combine remaining ¼ cup milk with coffee, ⅓ cup sugar, and egg yolks in a heavy saucepan. Cook over low heat, stirring constantly, until mixture is slightly thickened, about 10 minutes.

Remove the saucepan from the heat. Add the gelatin mixture and return the saucepan to the low heat. Stir the custard until all the gelatin has dissolved, then remove it from the heat and stir in the vanilla and cinnamon. Chill the custard until it is the consistency of unbeaten egg white, about 25 minutes.

Place the water in a metal bowl; freeze for 25 minutes or until a thin layer of ice forms on the surface. Meanwhile, beat the egg whites until foamy; gradually add 3 of the 5 tablespoons of sugar and continue beating until stiff peaks form. Set aside.

Add the milk powder to the partially frozen water and beat at high speed with an electric mixer for 5 minutes or until stiff peaks form. Gently stir half the egg whites into the chilled custard; fold in the rest of the egg whites and the whipped milk. Pour this mixture into the prepared crust and chill until firm, about 3 hours.

Place the pecans and the remaining 2 tablespoons of sugar in a small skillet with a nonstick surface over medium-high heat. Stir the pecans and sugar until the sugar melts and coats the pecans. Remove the skillet from the heat and let the pecans cool. Break apart the pecans and sprinkle them on top of the pie. Store the pie in the refrigerator.

Serves 8 to 10

WATERMELON ICE

A porch swing soothes me like a grown-up cradle. Rocking back and forth in the sunshine, I can listen to those chains creak and pop for hours. It's an ideal place to soak up some peace of mind, or just to eat a big juicy piece of watermelon.

This watermelon ice is a cool way to enjoy a summer treat without juice dripping down your arm or seeds to slow you down.

2 *tablespoons water*	**1** *cup cantaloupe pulp*
2 *tablespoons sugar*	
2 *cups watermelon pulp, seeded*	

Place the water and sugar in a small saucepan over medium-high heat. Cook, stirring until the sugar is well dissolved, about 5 minutes. Remove from the heat and let cool.

Place the fruit pulp and cooled syrup in a blender or food processor and process until very smooth. Freeze in an ice-cream freezer according to manufacturer's instructions.

Makes about 3 cups

SPICED PECAN DROP COOKIES

When I turned seven years old, my mother gave a "play lady" tea party in my honor. At four that afternoon, my female class-mates and cousins gathered in the dance hall at the Natchez Country Club dressed like cast members from *What Ever Happened to Baby Jane?* and *Hush ... Hush, Sweet Charlotte.* I greeted my guests in my mother's lavender chiffon tea dress, my great-grandmother's enormous straw hat, and entirely too much red lipstick.

The party decorations included petite tables set with linen nap-kins, tea sets, and tea trays with cream puffs, tiny peanut butter and jelly sandwiches, and meringue cookies. The afternoon passed like a little girl's dream as we paired off with our best friends, scrutinizing each other's outfits and trying to sip Coca-Cola from tin teacups in our mothers' oversize gloves. Since then, I have attended many grown-up tea parties; however, I've never noticed much of a difference.

Serve these guilt-free cookies at teatime. They won't spoil a girl's supper or her waistline.

3 egg whites	Scant teaspoon ground
1½ cups sifted light brown sugar	cinnamon
1 cup ground pecans	Scant teaspoon grated nutmeg
1 teaspoon vanilla extract	

Preheat the oven to 325 degrees. Spray a cookie sheet with nonstick vegetable coating and dust lightly with flour.

Whip the egg whites until soft peaks form. Add the brown sugar very slowly, about 2 tablespoons at a time, beating constantly. Fold in the ground pecans, vanilla, and spices. Drop the batter from a teaspoon, spacing well apart, onto the prepared pan. Bake for 20 minutes. Cool in the pan.

Makes 50 1½-inch wafers

PEACH RICE PUDDING

The peaches add a fresh taste to this light version of an old favorite.

1½ *cups skim milk*
⅓ *cup sugar*
3 *whole eggs plus 1 egg white*

½ *cup cooked white rice*
⅔ *cup chopped fresh peaches*
1 *teaspoon vanilla extract*

Preheat the oven to 250 degrees. Spray a 1-quart baking dish or loaf pan with nonstick vegetable coating.

Scald the milk in a small saucepan over medium-high heat and add the sugar. Remove the saucepan from the heat and stir until the sugar is well dissolved. Let this mixture cool.

Beat the whole eggs and egg white until well blended. Slowly stir the beaten eggs into the cooled milk and sugar mixture, add the remaining ingredients, and stir well. Pour the batter into the prepared pan. Place the pan in a larger pan and pour in boiling water half way up the sides of the batter-filled pan. Bake the pudding for 45 minutes or until firm. Serve hot.

Serves 8

GINGERBREAD

~~~~~~~~~~~~~~~~~~

This is a rich and flavorful cake which is absolutely delicious, either hot out of the oven or served cold.

½ cup canola oil
½ cup sugar
1 egg, beaten
2½ cups all-purpose flour
1½ teaspoons baking soda
1 teaspoon ground ginger

1 teaspoon ground cinnamon
½ teaspoon salt
1 cup frozen apple juice concentrate, thawed
1 cup molasses (see Note)

Spray a 10-inch Bundt pan with nonstick vegetable coating.

Beat together the oil, sugar, and egg in a large bowl until fluffy and very light yellow. Set aside. In a separate bowl, sift together the dry ingredients. Set aside.

Heat the apple juice concentrate over high heat to the boiling point and stir in the molasses. Add the dry ingredients and the molasses mixture alternately to the egg mixture until well blended. Pour into the prepared pan and bake for 40 minutes.

Cool in the pan for 10 minutes, then turn out onto a cake rack and cool completely or serve warm.

Serves 10 to 12

Note: If you do not like the flavor of molasses, try substituting honey.

BLACKBERRY MOUSSE

~~~~~~~~~~~~~~~~~~

This dessert may also be made with strawberries or blueberries.

1 pound fresh blackberries
½ cup sugar

1 tablespoon rum
¼ teaspoon ground cinnamon

2 packages unflavored gelatin	**5** egg whites
1 cup plain yogurt (see Note) or light sour cream	

Press the berries through a fine sieve or food mill to puree and remove the seeds. You should have about 1¼ cups of puree. Place 1 cup of the puree, sugar, rum, and cinnamon in a saucepan over low heat and cook, stirring, until the sugar is dissolved, about 10 minutes.

Sprinkle the gelatin over the remaining ¼ cup puree and let stand 1 minute. Stir the gelatin into the hot mixture and stir to dissolve completely. Place in the refrigerator to cool for 30 minutes.

Beat the yogurt or sour cream into the cooled berry mixture. Beat the egg whites until soft peaks form and fold them into the berry mixture. Spoon the mousse into six 1-cup dessert glasses or a 1½-quart decorative bowl, and refrigerate for at least 6 hours before serving.

Serves 6

Note: When cooking with yogurt, find a brand that has a creamy, custardlike consistency. Try to avoid a watery yogurt. You are more likely to find good-quality yogurt in a health food store.

BUTTERMILK SHERBET

If you like the flavor of cheesecake, you'll like this sherbet.

1 quart buttermilk	Pinch of salt
1 cup evaporated skim milk	**1** cup sugar
7 tablespoons fresh lemon juice	**1** teaspoon vanilla extract

Mix all the ingredients in a large bowl. Pour into an ice-cream freezer and freeze according to the manufacturer's instructions.

Makes about 1 quart

CHOCOLATE ANGEL FOOD CAKE

The chocolate gives this delicate cake plenty of flavor but its light texture will make you feel like you could eat a second helping of dessert. I always do.

¾ cup sifted cake flour
¼ cup cocoa
Whites of 14 large eggs
¼ teaspoon salt

1 teaspoon cream of tartar
1 teaspoon vanilla extract
1½ cups sifted sugar

Preheat the oven to 350 degrees.

Sift the cake flour with the cocoa 4 times; set aside.

In a large bowl, beat the egg whites until foamy. Add the salt, cream of tartar and vanilla and continue to beat the whites until soft peaks form.

Fold the sugar into the beaten egg whites a tablespoon at a time, then sift the cocoa mixture over the egg whites and fold in. Turn the batter into an ungreased 10-inch tube pan. Bake for 45 to 50 minutes.

When the cake is done, invert the pan on a rack and allow the cake to cool while still in the pan. Run a knife between the cake and the edge of the pan to remove the cake from the pan. If you do not have an angel food cake cutter, insert 2 forks into the cake, back to back, and gently pull slices apart.

Serves 10 to 12

STRAWBERRY SHERBET

This sherbet is mostly berries and has a luscious strawberry taste.

1 pint fresh strawberries,
  washed and hulled
½ cup honey

½ cup evaporated skim
  milk
2 tablespoons lemon juice

Place all the ingredients in a blender or food processor and process until very smooth. Freeze in an ice-cream freezer according to manufacturer's directions.

Makes 2 pints

MAMA LADY'S ONE-LAYER SPICE CAKE

Serve this simple cake with whole fresh fruit or a fruit puree.

1 cup light brown sugar, packed
1 cup boiling water
1 cup raisins
⅓ cup margarine
1½ teaspoon baking powder
1½ cups all-purpose flour
¼ teaspoon grated nutmeg
1 teaspoon ground cinnamon

Pinch of ground cloves
¼ teaspoon ground ginger
¼ teaspoon ground allspice
½ teaspoon salt
1½ teaspoons vanilla extract
Confectioners' sugar, for decoration

Preheat the oven to 350 degrees. Spray an 8-inch round cake pan with nonstick vegetable coating.

Place the brown sugar, water, raisins, and margarine in a small saucepan over medium heat and bring to the boil. Cook, stirring until the sugar is completely dissolved, about 5 minutes. Set aside to cool.

Sift together the baking powder, flour, spices, and salt. Pour the cooled sugar mixture into a large bowl. Beat in the flour mixture a little at a time until well blended. Stir in the vanilla. Pour into the prepared pan and bake for 45 minutes. Cool on a rack and garnish with confectioners' sugar.

Serves 8

Pecan-Honey Candy

This Christmas candy is easy to make for a gift or to keep around the kitchen and serve with hot wassail, eggnog, or coffee.

3½ cups coarsely chopped pecans

1 cup honey

¼ teaspoon ground cinnamon

¼ teaspoon grated nutmeg

¼ teaspoon ground cloves

2 teaspoons salt, or to taste

Preheat the oven to 350 degrees.

Spread the pecans on a nonstick baking sheet and roast for about 10 minutes or until fragrant.

In a 2-quart saucepan, bring the honey to a boil, stir in the toasted pecans and spices, and cook over medium-high heat, stirring constantly, for 10 minutes. Spoon the candy onto a wet wooden chopping board and shape into a ½-inch-thick rectangle. When it is thoroughly cooled, cut into strips and then into diamonds. Salt to taste.

Makes about 2 dozen pieces

Sweet Potato Cake with Ricotta Filling

*The ricotta cream makes this cake tall and fluffy and the sweet
potatoes keep it moist and creamy.*

1½ cups canola oil

2 cups sugar

4 eggs, separated

½ cup hot water

1 tablespoon baking
powder

¼ teaspoon salt

1¼ teaspoons ground
cinnamon

½ teaspoon ground ginger

½ teaspoon grated nutmeg

½ teaspoon ground cloves

1½ cups grated peeled sweet
potato (about 1 large
sweet potato)

1 cup chopped pecans

1 teaspoon vanilla extract

Ricotta Filling

2½ pounds skim-milk
ricotta

1 teaspoon vanilla extract

1½ cups confectioners'
sugar

Preheat the oven to 350 degrees. Spray three 8-inch round cake pans
with nonstick vegetable coating.

Combine the oil and sugar in a large bowl and beat with an electric
mixer until smooth. Add the egg yolks one at a time, beating well after
each addition. Stir in the hot water.

Sift together the dry ingredients and mix into the batter. The batter will
become quite stiff. Stir in the sweet potatoes, pecans, and vanilla. Beat
the egg whites until soft peaks form. Fold the egg whites into the batter.

Divide the batter among the prepared pans and bake for 25 to 30
minutes, until a toothpick inserted in center comes out clean or until
the cakes bounce back after a slight poke with your finger. Cool the
layers on wire racks before stacking with the ricotta filling.

For the filling, beat together all ingredients with an electric mixer until
very smooth. Spread between the layers and on the top of the cake.

Serves 10 to 12

SWEET POTATO PIE

The manipulation of a few added egg whites takes plain old sweet potato pie to new heights.

Crust

¾ cup ground pecans

¾ cup graham cracker crumbs

½ cup light brown sugar, packed

½ teaspoon ground cinnamon

½ teaspoon grated nutmeg

2 tablespoons (¼ stick) margarine, melted

Filling

2 cups pureed cooked sweet potato

2 tablespoons molasses

¼ cup light brown sugar, packed

½ teaspoon vanilla extract

¼ teaspoon ground cinnamon

¼ teaspoon grated nutmeg

¼ teaspoon ground ginger

3 egg whites

Meringue Topping

2 egg whites

¼ teaspoon cream of tartar

3 tablespoons granulated sugar, sifted

To make the crust, mix all the ingredients with a fork or your hands, making sure the dry ingredients are well dampened with the margarine. Press very firmly into the bottom and sides of an 8-inch springform pan or 8-inch deep-dish pie pan. Place the crust in the freezer while you make the filling.

Preheat the oven to 375 degrees.

To make the filling, beat the sweet potato puree with the molasses, brown sugar, vanilla, and spices. In a separate bowl, beat the egg whites until soft peaks form. Fold these egg whites into the sweet potato mixture. Pour the batter into the prepared crust and bake the pie for 30 minutes or until a knife inserted in the center comes out clean. Remove the pie from the oven and reduce the temperature to 325 degrees.

To make the topping, beat the egg whites until foamy and add the cream of tartar. Continue to beat the whites, sprinkling in the granulated sugar until soft peaks form and egg whites are shiny. Spread the meringue on top of the pie and bake for another 10 minutes, or until the meringue is lightly browned. Cool in a draft-free place, but not the refrigerator.

Serves 12

BANANA CREAM PIE

~~~~~~

The custard, bananas, and cookies can also be layered and served as an old-fashioned banana pudding.

¼ cup sugar	½ teaspoon vanilla extract
1½ tablespoons cornstarch	4 cups sliced ripe bananas
¼ cup skim milk, cool, plus 1¾ cups scalded	2 tablespoons lemon juice
2 egg yolks	1 tablespoon honey
⅛ teaspoon cream of tartar	32 vanilla wafers
1 tablespoon dark rum	2 tablespoons (¼ stick) margarine, melted

Fill the bottom of a double boiler with water and bring to a simmer over medium-high heat. In the top of the double boiler (not yet over heat), combine the sugar and cornstarch. In a separate bowl, lightly beat together the ¼ cup milk and egg yolks. Gradually add the egg mixture to the sugar and cornstarch and stir until well dissolved. Add the scalded milk, cream of tartar, and rum, stirring constantly. Place over boiling water and stir constantly until smooth and thick (about 15 minutes). Remove from heat, stir in vanilla, and cool.

Toss the banana slices with the lemon and honey; set aside.

Crush the cookies in a food processor or between 2 sheets of wax paper with a rolling pin. Place the cookie crumbs and melted margarine in a 9-inch pie pan; mix well with your hands or a fork, making sure the crumbs are well moistened, then press firmly into the bottom and sides of the pan. Chill the crust thoroughly before filling.

Spread cooled custard into the pie crust. Drain the banana slices and arrange them (overlapping) in concentric circles on top of the custard. Cover and chill thoroughly before serving.

Serves 8

INDEX

Grateful acknowledgment is made for permission to reprint the following photographs:
Pages xiii, 20, 33, 70, 74, 109, 115, 129, 151, 168 from the collection of Elena Z. Carter. Pages x, xiv, xv, 8, 105, 116, 120, 157, 179 from the

PHOTOGRAPH CREDITS

collection of Hattie Ruder. Pages 27, 62 from the collection of Mrs. Charles Everette Ratcliffe. Pages ii, vi, viii, xvi, 5, 14, 34, 50, 54, 66, 73, 86, 90, 97, 102, 125, 134, 143, 154, 170, 184 courtesy of Mississippi Department of Archives and History.